TREAD OF THE LONGHORNS

TREAD OF THE LONGHORNS

BY WALTER GANN

ILLUSTRATIONS BY R. L. MCCOLLISTER

CUTTING EDGE

ISBN-13: 978-1-954840-33-1

Published by
Cutting Edge Books
PO Box 8212
Calabasas, CA 91372
www.cuttingedgebooks.com

To the memory of the old time cowmen,
some of whom were my friends
and counsellors

TREAD OF THE LONGHORNS

CONTENTS

FOREWORD

THERE is romance even in the title of Walter Gann's book, TREAD OF THE LONGHORNS, and the content of this early-day picture backs the promise. It is the story of cattle from the earliest days until the time when the flood of Texas cows had burst the bounds of the Lone Star State, taken the northern trail, and found a home in every valley of that vast tract which became known as Cattleland.

This is not a formal history with a thousand footnotes. It is full of incidents that have the color of life. It is the story of history at the source. You cannot read it without understanding better the character of the West, since cattle were so great a factor in building it. Its laws, social customs, habits of life, were all tremendously modified by the Texas trail drives and the subsequent establishment of ranches in its domain.

Nobody but Walter Gann could have written this book. Texas born, he was astride a bronco, riding with his father on a cattle drive, at the age of five. Before he was ten, he was a good cowhand in the making. By the time he was fifteen he could "ride 'em slick" when the bucker went sunfishing. He punched cows on the Concho and the Pecos. In the summers of 1908 and 1909 he worked the Yellowstone and the Powder rivers in Montana. And he handled cattle for himself and others in Western Kansas.

If all that experience does not entitle Gann to know cows and write about them, nothing could. He looks and talks like a cowman. It is bred in his bone. What is more to the point, he writes like one. He brings back to us vividly the dust of the drag drive and the winds of the plains, the fretting of cattle, and all the unforgettable memories of a period that has gone forever.

— WILLIAM MACLEOD RAINE

CHAPTER ONE
THE HEAD OF A COW

CATTLE are just about as old as any of our domestic animals. The business of raising them is just about as old as any industry on record. Men have been at it since the days of Abraham, and it is still with us in a vigorous and healthy way. One does not read many pages in the Book of Genesis, recounting the dark days of early history, until incidents of herdsmen and their troubles spread themselves upon the pages. Many problems which the cattlemen faced during that day and time are with them now.

The Bible speaks of drouths and feed shortages and diseases among the herds. There were strife and disagreements over range and water rights not greatly different from those that occurred in this country not so many years ago. Sharp-witted persons preyed upon the gullibility and misfortunes of those early-day cowmen in much the same manner that has been practiced here. There is an account of certain unscrupulous individuals who took advantage of Father Abraham's disturbed condition of mind over the death of his beloved Sarah and compelled him to sacrifice many head of his stock for a given amount of silver shekels to pay the funeral expenses.

There is nothing said in the Bible about theft of cattle as we know of it today, but it seems that anyone engaged in the business during Biblical times needed to be on the alert to protect his interests. As an example, Jacob tried to pull a fast one on Laban when he indulged in a little scenery-shifting to further his own gains.

Jacob was running the herds of his wife's father on shares. That kind of arrangement is practiced more or less in America between the owners of the stock and the caretakers to this day. In the case of Jacob and his partner, the basis for division of the profits was unique and it is out-of-date at this writing. Jacob's share of the increase was to be all off-colored animals, such as spotted and ring-streaked calves. With the agreement in force, he set out to create a condition that would guarantee him his full share.

As a pre-natal influence upon prospective mothers to mark their calves, he blazed spots upon all tree trunks around the watering places. He stripped bark from the shrubbery and laid freshly peeled limbs in the water troughs. No matter which way a cow let her gaze wander when she made her daily trip to the well for a drink, there was reflected back into her eyes a setting of spots, specks and streaks. Just how profitable this ingenious method might have been is not known because the perpetrator was detected in other tricky work before the scheme got a fair trial, and he was compelled to flee before the wrath of his father-in-law.

From those ancient accounts, cattle were handled in fairly large numbers, but it seems that they were held closely and constantly under herd. Nothing is said about their wandering around over large areas to be gathered again; and there is nothing to suggest that anything resembling a roundup was ever held. There is nothing in history about large herds of cattle being handled in any other country at a later date, and it was not until after the discovery and settlement of America that great numbers of them were found together again. While the cattle business of early Biblical times comes in for much prominence, it pales before the glorious light of the American era.

Here, a great industry grew up purely by accident, and it was ready for exploitation when discovered. No epoch in world history produced the romance and glamor that surrounded, and still clings to, the early cattle trade. No other enterprise ever gathered such a set of picturesque characters as those who rode the range upon their roundup circles and followed the great herds over the long miles of trail. No star ever flared so brightly and dimmed so quickly. The true romantic period of the cattle business came and went in fifty years, and there are a few men living today who saw the beginning and the end.

The industry still exists on a large scale with more money invested in it than ever before, but a different class of men is now carrying it onward. It is being conducted in a modern, business-like manner, and a much better grade of beef is being produced than ever before, but the romance is dead. The present-day cowboy is working under safer and pleasanter conditions than those who preceded him, but he has lost much of his right of self-assertion and much of his independence. There is little about the calling today that would lure a boy away from a comfortable home to undergo the dangers of a cowboy's life or that would hold him after he got there. The work is conducted in a planned and machine-like order, and it is not without an element of drudgery.

In America, this mammoth industry spread itself over an area greater than all the lands of Abraham, Isaac, Jacob, and Joseph combined. Millions of cattle grew wild, and they were controlled by thousands of men riding tens of thousands of horses. Nothing like this had ever been undertaken. There was no set pattern to serve as a guide for this gigantic problem, and those engaged in the calling had to work out and devise their own system. They were compelled to deal with the forces of nature and take the kind of weather that came to them; and they had to learn how to interpret the instinctive moods of the wild animals they controlled. The handling of cattle grew into an art of high technique, and to the Texans belongs the glory of its perfection.

The large-scale, open-range cattle industry began with poorly equipped and undermanned outfits along the Gulf Coast and the Rio Grande in the late Sixties. It ended amid a fanfare of color and romance in the great Northwest at the Canadian border. There was little comparison between the elaborate and highly organized combinations of the Montana roundups and the poverty-stricken cow-hunting expeditions of Texas. The first Texas outfits were ill rationed and sadly underpaid, while the Montana cowboys enjoyed the best of food and the highest wages ever paid in open-range cattle history.

The Scotch were the first to drive cattle over a stretch of any distance. They came down from the bleak Highlands of their country, with their small bunches, to the markets of Glasgow, London and Liverpool. A great deal has been written in both song and story about those first drovers, but there is nothing in common between them and the American cowboys. Scotch cattle were gentle, and hand raised in small bunches, and their owners drove them to market on foot. An American cowboy would never have indulged in such servitude. He was a gentleman on horseback and proud and jealous of his station.

On their periodical trips to market, the jolly Scotsmen are pictured in prose and poetry as sitting around tables in taverns at night, drinking ale and indulging in song and levity, with their small droves of animals conveniently penned in nearby paddocks. While the Scotch cowboys enjoyed whatever entertainment the grogshops had to offer, the Americans were holding a thousand or more wild cattle in a single herd, riding in the rain and darkness with one eye upon their restless charges and the other cocked for the approach of hostile Indians.

The large-scale cattle business in America was started entirely by accident. Those responsible for its beginning had no idea of the greatness that was to follow. A series of other occurrences extremely remote from the scene and subject touched upon it and wielded a strong influence in its development.

In faraway New England, two Yankee gunsmiths experimenting with firearms played an important part. One of them was Samuel Colt, who made the first practical revolver that could shoot six times without reloading. This wonderful gun, which came to be known the country over as the six-shooter, turned the tide of battle in favor of the Texas Rangers against the hostile Indians, and it enabled the cowboys to hold the meager footing the Rangers gave them. The other inventor was Oliver Winchester, who came out with the first repeating rifle and its metallic cartridge. This modern gun not only served as an effective weapon against the Indians, but it also was instrumental in destroying the buffalo, which was the Indian's main source of food.

While the invention of weapons contributed to the development of the cattle industry, other factors far removed played an important part. A Frenchman in Paris, experimenting with an instrument that could pound a small hole deep in the earth, made his contribution when he invented the first deep-well machine.

Thus, when all available land watered by natural streams was fully stocked, the deep well brought millions of acres of dry land into use.

But a small hole in the ground, some six inches in diameter and from fifty to three hundred feet in depth, was of little use, even if it did tap an unlimited source of water. Means had to be devised to get water on top of the ground in fairly large quantities, at a reasonable cost, before it would benefit a range country. Up in Wisconsin, this problem was solved by a dairy farmer when he developed a contraption that could draw water from a deep well in large amounts, with no more power than the wind itself. Thus, in time, the Frenchman's deep-well machine and the dairy farmer's windmill were employed on a gigantic scale in the arid range lands of America. This combination brought large areas of grassland within easy reach of a grazing cow.

Until the late Seventies, cattle ran wild and mingled together. Inbreeding was running free, and the animals were not improving in quality. Some range men longed for an improved breed, but no individual could afford to furnish high-priced breeding stock and have all his neighbors benefit at his expense. While the cattlemen of the far flung range country were seeking a solution to their problem, an Illinois farmer was solving it for them.

In 1874 the manufacture of the first barbed wire for fencing was begun. Within a few years the Texas cowmen were fencing their ranges, and a steady improvement in the quality of their cattle developed when better-grade animals were imported into the country for breeding purposes. As with the windmill, a market for barbed wire arose in this remote area, far beyond the dreams of its inventor.

Since Texas was the cradle of the open-range cattle industry, it would appear that Providence had a hand in its selection. No other country in the world was superior to the hills and prairies of Texas for breeding and growing livestock. The pure water and abundant grasses insured the healthy growth of a young animal.

The mild climate prevented heavy death losses during the winter, at the time when cattle had to look to their own foraging for a living.

In the early dawn of Texas history, the province was claimed by both Spain and France. Each country sought to bolster its claim by attempts at settlement. In this, Spain was the more persistent and, eventually, the more successful. It was during these incursions by representatives of the Spanish Crown that the seed for the vast cattle herds were sown. By the same manner the foundation for the wild horses which grew up with cattle was started. Among the series of chance happenings relating to the cattle industry, this was the most remarkable accident of them all.

Never before in history were horses needed so greatly and employed so widely. And here they were — just like the cattle — all ready for use. Experience has proven that a certain type of horse was best adapted for handling wild cattle. Here again, it looks as though Providence had a hand in shaping affairs. Those descendants of the Spanish cavalry horses, which grew up in the open-range country, could not have been better for their mission if they had been ordered solely for that purpose. Horses played such a vital and important role in cattle history that they deserve a separate chapter in this work, and the subject will be treated at a later time.

When the Spaniards marched into Texas more than four hundred years ago, they had no thought of starting the vast cattle industry. They were hunting gold and jewel treasures, and when they failed to see the huge possibilities of the cattle trade, they overlooked far greater riches than they could otherwise have hoped to find.

Before the middle of the sixteenth century, the Spanish started two expeditions of exploration and conquest with Texas as their goal. The first was launched in 1528 under the command of Pánfilo de Narváez. The other was led by Hernando de Soto, some ten or twelve years later. Both expeditions used Florida as a starting base, and both were to be a joint land and sea operation. Both had the misfortune to become lost from their supply ships, and both were dismal failures. Both forces suffered unbearable hardships from sickness and hunger and Indian depredations, and both commanders sacrificed their lives to the venture. From the Narváez force of four hundred men (and many horses) only four men survived. These succeeded in reaching Texas and, eventually, the Spanish settlements in Mexico. Neither of the aforementioned expeditions had any bearing upon the livestock industry of America, but a peculiar circumstance in relation to one of the survivors is worth mentioning.

The first white man to set foot on Texas soil and live to tell about it, was the Spaniard Alvar Nuñez Cabeza de Vaca. He was the treasurer of the ill-fated Narváez Expedition. A long series of misfortunes followed the company, finally bringing them to the necessity of of killing all their horses for food. In a final and desperate attempt to reach the Spanish settlements in Mexico, they set out upon the Gulf, from where they were stranded upon the east bank of the Mississippi. All of the boats became lost, but Cabeza de Vaca landed upon a small island in what was later to be known as Galveston Bay. His companions died of hunger and privations. Cabeza de Vaca managed to make the mainland alone, but he was immediately taken prisoner by the Indians. For seven years, this proud representative of the Spanish Crown, who bore a title conferred upon the family by the king three hundred years before, led the degrading life of a slave to the heathen Indians.

His enforced captivity took him up and down the Gulf Coast, and inland to the edge of what he later called the Buffalo Plains. When at last he encountered three other members of the expedition who had embarked in a different boat, the four succeeded in escaping from their Indian captors. They managed to make their painful way across the Rio Grande to their own people in Mexico.

Cabeza de Vaca wrote extensively of his experiences and observations in the New World, but he said nothing about cattle in any of his writings. He spoke of seeing buffalo on one of his trips into Central Texas, but he never mentioned horses in his account from the time the last ones were slain for food until he encountered the band of his fellow countrymen in Mexico. Since so many odd circumstances surround the cattle industry, it is fitting to say a few more words with reference to Cabeza de Vaca.

Three centuries before, a progenitor of his by the name of Martín Alhaja, was a simple sheepherder in the mountain wilderness of Spain. During one of the Moorish wars, Martín performed a valuable service to his country by directing the Spanish Army over a secret pass in the Pyrenees, which maneuver allowed them to outflank the enemy. He marked the entrance to the pass by placing the skull of a cow in the road at the turning-off place. As a reward, the king ennobled the sheepherder and all his descendants. He conferred upon Martín Alhaja the title of Cabeza de Vaca.

At the time of his sojourn in America, Alvar Nuñez was the rightful and legal heir to that title. It is strikingly peculiar that the first white man to tread the soil of what was destined to be the greatest cattle country in all the world, bore the full name and title of Alvar Nuñez Cabeza de Vaca. Translated into English, Cabeza de Vaca means head of a cow.

While Cabeza de Vaca was being held captive by the Texas Indians, another grand expedition of conquest was launched. It was also sponsored by the Spanish Crown, but it used Mexico as a starting point. It was led by the Spanish nobleman, Francisco Vásquez de Coronado. It was planned to be far-reaching in scope, and the force consisted of several hundred mounted soldiers, with a large complement of slave baggage carriers and livestock herders, amounting to nearly a thousand people. They drove some six or eight hundred cattle and three thousand sheep. From the standpoint of an exploration the undertaking was a partial success, but as a conquest it was a failure.

Coronado established headquarters upon the Rio Grande in north central New Mexico and made side trips of exploration from there. At first he secured help from the native Indians, but after they caught onto the traditional treachery of the Spanish, they turned enemy and harassed the invaders almost to the point of destruction. In spite of the Indian hostility, Coronado was able to sojourn in their midst for three years, and return to his starting place with most of his men, but with a very small proportion of his livestock.

This episode is mentioned only because some authorities credit the Coronado Expedition with sowing the seed that was to produce the great herds of wild cattle and horses in America, but there is little or no support for this theory. Undoubtedly Coronado lost much of his livestock during those three desperate years, but there is no evidence that any of these animals ever reached the breeding grounds of southern Texas. The Indians learned that both cow and horse meat were edible, and there is good reason to believe that the few animals that were not consumed by Coronado and his force were later eaten by the Indians. The region occupied by Coronado was not the natural habitat of the buffalo, and it is easy to see that the Indians would prefer to slay straying horses and cows rather than journey to the buffalo plains for their food.

There is one thing that impressed all those first invading Spaniards. They learned at heavy cost that the Indians of North America were an entirely different breed from those encountered south of the Isthmus. Both Alvar Nuñez and the recorder for the De Soto Expedition commented widely upon the fierceness of the North American Indian, with the conclusion that the country could not be conquered and held short of a long and bloody war. Coronado did not need to draw any conclusions. He knew from experience, and the report of his expedition told the entire story. Those invaders encountered in North America the air that carries the breath of freedom and independence. It seemed to stir men's souls and give them strength and determination for greater deeds. This was the environment that was later to mold the character of the American cowboy.

For nearly a hundred years, no Spaniards ventured north of the Rio Grande. The next incursion was undertaken by the church with the avowed purpose of converting the heathen Indians to Christianity. It was led by Juan de Salas and Diego Ortega, two Catholic friars, but hiding behind their robes was a strong force of soldiers. This expedition also carried a body of slave baggage carriers and herders. The number of livestock is not mentioned in the account, but from the far reaching plans of the expedition, it must have been considerable.

The expedition crossed the Rio Grande and moved in a northeasterly direction for two hundred miles above the mouth of what was later to became known as the Colorado River. The friars' written reports back to headquarters were not at all encouraging. They were able to induce only a very few Indians into the fold, and these seemed to believe that salvation was the end of all strife. After attaching themselves to the expedition, they acted as though their only mission in life were to rest easy and consume food supplied by those wonderful men from across the sea.

But the good friars gave a more vivid account of another class of Indians who were altogether different. These latter tribesmen, who later became known as the Comanches and Apaches, defied those messengers of God and their bodyguard of soldiers. They lurked in the brush of canyon and river bottoms and carried on an unrelenting warfare of ambush against the invaders. They exhibited little respect for or fear of those self-styled great men who rode strange animals that could run with the speed of the wind, and whose weapons roared their anger like the thunder. Between the Indian beggars who continually dogged their footsteps and the savage fighters who took their daily toll of death from the expedition, the friars were at last forced to acknowledge failure and return to Mexico after a year of wasted effort. While most of the personnel returned, they left many head of their livestock.

In 1634 an army captain by name of Alfonso Vaca, a cousin of the ill-fortuned Cabeza de Vaca, led a much larger force of invaders over the same route. About all he seems to have accomplished was to sink deeper into the country than the timid friars had done. He was also greatly harassed by the Indians, and he frankly stated in the report of his sojourn that he lost many livestock. He laid the blame upon the slave herders who he says were too lazy to keep a close watch upon the animals and prevent them from straying, and then were too cowardly to attempt their recovery. He gave no explanation as to why he and his brave soldiers did not seek to recover the strayed animals.

Those Spanish soldiers who made up the military units were purely adventurers in search of wealth for their Crown and personal glory for themselves. They classed themselves as *caballeros,* or gentlemen on horseback, who would never degrade themselves by caring for an animal. That was the work of the *mozos,* or despised Indian slaves. The *conquistadores* were strictly fighting men, and when not in battle, they lived a life of ease, which included riotous drinking sprees and lengthy *siestas* to rid themselves of the hangovers.

Even so, the slaves had their moments of relaxation too. While their masters were indulging in drunken orgies, they seized upon the opportunity to secure some well-deserved rest for themselves. It was during these periods that the ball was started to rolling. While the haughty soldiers slept in drunken stupors and the slave herders slept from pure exhaustion, the herds went unattended. It was only natural that many head of both horses and cattle should stray from the main bunches. Once they reached the cover of brush thicket or river bottom, they were usually safe from recovery.

Those simple-minded slaves had learned that death lurked in every hidden spot for those who ventured too far from the main camp. They could recall the cries of their brothers who had been so unfortunate as to fall victims of the crafty foe which glided through the brush like snakes, ready to strike on sight. Those unconverted Indians had a special kind of cruel torture for members of their own race who had degraded themselves for the privilege of serving those treacherous men who pretended to have a new and wonderful God. Rather than risk death by torture, the fearful slaves would let the straying animals go unsought and accept the punishment of their masters.

Even the brave *conquistadores* had learned the kind of death song the whistling Comanche arrows carried. They had also seen the bloody heads of their dead companions after the Indians had lifted their scalps. They had no more stomach for risking hair and hide than the lowly slaves, and certainly a few head of horses or cattle were not worth the price of their own lives. They would even things up by taking out their spite upon the lazy herders. Thus, a few animals lost here, and a few lost there, some from one expedition and some from another, would in the end make a sizable bunch. With natural instinct to guide them, it is not difficult to see these straying animals uniting in small bunches for mating. Leave them alone for two hundred years, and it is no strain upon the imagination to visualize the enormity of their increase.

Other attempts were made, first by the church and then the military, to get a foothold in the new land during the following fifty years, but they all failed. France made one feeble attempt to assert claim to the new country, but that also ended in failure. Three shiploads of colonists which landed on the Gulf disappeared in a mysterious manner, and no one ever knew their fate. After this, France withdrew from the contest and left Spain with an undisputed claim to the country.

In 1689 another expedition was started by the Spaniards. The purpose of this one was permanent settlement, and it carried some promise of success. There were many families and many head of livestock, with the soldiers furnishing bodily protection and the friars dispensing spiritual guidance. The people were to make homes in the regions best adapted for stock growing, while the military was to establish a line of forts between them and the Indian tribes. Then the friars were to take up where others left off and make side trips into the Indian country to convert the Indians to Christianity. Records kept by members of the expedition state that they were surprised to encounter many small bunches of wild cattle after crossing the Rio Grande. But their greatest surprise was to find the Indians mounted on horses and ready to give battle.

The following year, another large body of colonists joined the first one, bringing along their herds of breeding stock and the protective soldiers. It was soon discovered that not only had the Indians learned to make use of horses for warfare and transportation, but they had learned other tricks as well. Many complaints were received at headquarters that the Indians were busily engaged in stealing horses belonging to the settlers. One of the friars recorded in his writings that, while wild horses seemed plentiful, the Indians preferred to steal the gentle animals rather than catch and tame the wild ones. Meetings of the settlers were held, and respectful requests were despatched to military headquarters for restoration of their property.

But the soldiers had their hands full too, and they found little time to recover stolen horses. They learned that a much abler and bolder enemy opposed them than in the days when Indians traveled on foot. From their old tricks of lying hidden in ambush they had developed entirely new tactics. They were mounted now and knew how to strike and run away. From their many encounters with this newly organized foe, the soldiers found that he was able to display something different in the art of warfare.

The friars also found a different class of people from what they expected. The Indians had increased greatly in pride and arrogance, and they were in no mood to listen to anyone in the name of Christianity. They had a good horse between their legs and were equipped with a splendid supply of bows and arrows and lances. The Indians had also learned the art of deception from the swashbuckling *conquistadores* of a century ago, and they indulged in its practice. With false pretenses of interest in the religion the friars expounded, they lured many of the priests to their deaths by coaxing them and their bodyguards of soldiers into the interior, where they were wantonly slaughtered.

Thus, in time the missionaries and settlers came to realize the dismal state of affairs. Many a peaceful *ranchero* and his family learned the sorrowful and fateful meaning of that blood-curdling yell which preceded a sweep of charging warriors upon a defenseless settlement at the break of dawn. Many massacres were committed and many lives were sacrificed in that bloody period between 1689 and 1693. Hopes of the settlers turned to despondency, and they cast many wistful glances toward that safety zone beyond the Rio Grande. At last their prayers were heard across the Atlantic, and without further ado, the King of Spain issued direct orders that all efforts at colonizing Texas must cease. Once again the Spaniards drew back into Mexico and left the country in undisputed possession of the Indians. It was a fiercer, and more savage array of warriors who followed the defeated colonists and soldiers to the banks of the river and watched them cross. The Texas Indians were mounted fighting men now, and were ready to challenge any comers.

For twenty more years Texas was left alone by the white men. For twenty more years, cattle and horses north of the Rio Grande increased undisturbed. There is no way to estimate how many were running loose during that time, but from later events, the number reached large proportions. On first thought, it might be supposed that the Indians would utilize these animals for food and exterminate them, but they did not. There is a good reason for their failure to do so.

Horses will thrive the same in captivity as when running wild. Therefore, the adoption of the horse as a means of transportation had no effect upon its reproduction. An entirely different set of conditions prevailed in the Texas country from those which had surrounded Coronado when he made his sojourn in New Mexico. This latter region was not the natural habitat of the buffalo, and the Indians were compelled to make long journeys to the Staked Plains east of the Pecos to find them. It is conceivable that they would consume the few animals that were lost by Coronado. On the other hand, the prairies of Texas were teeming with buffalo. Since this animal had always been the Indians' main food, it was only natural that it remain so. The acquisition of their meat supply became an easy matter since they had acquired the use of horses. Besides it was a most thrilling sport to ride alongside a running animal and shoot it down from the back of a horse.

Wild cattle have a tendency to seek refuge in rough and brushy land when disturbed from any cause. It was to be many years before the Indians were to master the art of cow hunting as the English-and Spanish-speaking cowboys were soon to do. Thus, it is easy to see why the Indians would slay their favorite meat animal, which invariably roamed the open prairies, rather than go into the brush and rough lands after cows. Therefore, they trained their horses both for warfare and buffalo hunting, and from that time onward, the Indians were never again hungry until the last of these animals had been slain.

The next and last, and what was to be the first successful effort by the Spaniards to colonize Texas came in 1713. By a preponderance of numbers and hard fighting, the military managed to clear a strip along the Gulf Coast and Rio Grande. From that time onward, the grip was not broken until the war for Texas independence more than a hundred years later. The newly arrived settlers found the country literally alive with wild horses and cattle, and chroniclers wrote extensively on the subject.

They also found Indians who had perfected the art of horsemanship and who created their own brand of warfare. For more than a hundred and fifty years, constant and bloody hostilities raged between the white men and the Plains Indians. It was as late as 1876 that the Custer Massacre took place on the Little Big Horn in Montana, and it was later still before all the warring tribes were subdued and quartered peacefully upon their different reservations.

CHAPTER TWO
THE RANGERS
CLEAR THE WAY

THE first English-speaking settlers came to Texas in 1821. It is true that other adventurers had preceded them, but the former had no idea of settling down and making homes. They were roving prospectors and trappers, whose only purpose was to take riches from the ground and streams and then leave the country when the visible supply was exhausted. Since the climate of Texas is not adapted to fur production and the terrain showed little or no promise of mineral wealth, these waves of nomadic treasure hunters soon moved on to other fields.

But those who came in 1821 had every intention of remaining and creating a sovereign state out of the wilderness. They were men with families and they showed good faith by bringing their families with them. It has been a historical tradition of Americans to seek cheap and fertile lands for their home sites. The government of Spain, which at that time held sovereignty over Texas, was much more liberal, and wiser, in the policy of land allotment to homesteaders than was the government of the United States. Thus, between the arrival of the first English-speaking people in 1821 and the year 1830, a heavy migration of citizens from the United States was under way. These were the forebears of future ranchers and cowboys, but no one realized it at the time.

These first settlers were farmers and they came to the country with no other thought than farming in mind. Because of favorable soil and climatic conditions for land cultivation and because of access to timber for building purposes, they secured their land grants in the eastern and southern parts of the province. For mutual protection, they banded together in small communities and formed their own local governments. Fortunately for them, the Indians of this area were friendly, in direct contrast to the fierce tribes farther west who had fought the Spaniards for three hundred years along the Mexican border. Had these people located their homes in the lands of the Comanches and Kiowas, it is doubtful if any of them would have lived for another year.

Those newly arrived immigrants from the United States could by no stretch of the imagination have been called cowmen, and they had no thought of ever engaging in the business. Like most farmers of that day, each family owned one or more milk cows and at least one yoke of oxen, and that was all. Those better off financially owned a few horses, but these animals were high in price and out of reach of the majority. Neither were horses considered of much importance by the rank and file.

There was a limited number of wild cattle inhabiting the region where the first Americans settled. Although there was a distant kinship between them and the Longhorns, these animals bore little resemblance to the great herds that ran wild through the brush and hills four hundred miles to the west. Both species had come from the same root, but three hundred years in sharply contrasted environment had molded them into entirely different strains. Both had originated in Spain and both had been transplanted to the American mainland by way of the West Indies. Indeed, the cattle business had flourished in a moderate way for three centuries in the Bahama Islands. Spanish ships called at West Indian ports to replenish their water and food supplies, of which the most important item was beef. [As a safeguard against spoilage, the meat was smoke-cured and dried before being taken on board ship. It was through this practice that the word "buccaneer" was coined. *"Boucan"* is the Caribbean native word for smoked or dried beef. Those who engaged in the undertaking of processing and curing the meat were commonly called *"boucaniers."* Through the English-speaking people's habit of butchering foreign words and phrases and spelling them as they sound, the word was corrupted to buccaneer, which in time erroneously became a general term applied to Spanish sailors. Buccaneers were not originally the swashbuckling freebooters and pirates that many people came to believe. Instead, they were a simple, hard-working people, who toiled long hours over smoky fires processing and curing meat for the daring seamen who sailed the Spanish Main.]

The Longhorn cattle reached Texas from Mexico. The dry nature of the country, where they traveled great distances to and from water, developed them into long-legged, thinbodied animals, with horns of unbelievable dimensions. Southeast Texas has never been a desirable habitat for cattle because of local and climatic conditions. The rainfall is heavy, the grass is washy and without nutritious strength as compared with the sun-cured grass of the prairie. The country at one time contained much swampland and was heavily infested with insects such as huge flies and mosquitoes, which was all contrary to the natural instincts and grazing habits of a range cow. There was nothing about the climate or the food to induce the Longhorns to leave the prairies of South and West Texas to penetrate the swamplands along the eastern border.

While these cattle of southeastern Texas were of Spanish stock, they came to that area by way of Florida. They were few in number, and they were not prolific. They had been brought to the adjacent country by French settlers in Louisiana, and, in their migration across the southern part of the United States, they changed little from their original state. They had mixed more or less with the few animals imported from other parts of the country, and inbreeding had not been so widespread during their journey, which took three hundred years to make.

While these cattle had little or no influence in forming the great herds that were to develop later, they were, nevertheless, the first wild cattle the English-speaking people encountered. They were quickly absorbed by tame cattle the settlers had brought along and the two strains formed a breed known as Texas cattle. Accounts show them to have been wilder and fiercer in their habits than was the breed that reached Texas by way of Mexico. A Longhorn was never known to attack a man without the provocation of being crowded or hemmed into a close place from which he could not escape. On the other hand, those descendants of Spanish cattle in East Texas, with their short and keen horns, have been known to seek battle with man of their own free will.

The first American settlers found that the wild Indians out on the frontier owned many horses but laid claim to no cows. Along the Rio Grande and around the missions, under protection of the army, a few Mexican ranchers were herding small bunches of cattle, but they were making little or no effort to expand the business. The only market available was down in the interior of Mexico, but the price was so cheap and the trip was so long and arduous that it was hardly worth the pay. The art of trail driving had not been developed, and it was only waiting for American ingenuity and resourcefulness to create it. Then the Mexican war for independence, against the mother country of Spain, broke out. This virtually stopped all traffic between the Texas colonists and the interior of Mexico.

The effects of this war would hardly have been felt among the English-speaking citizens of the province had it not been for the traditional adventurous spirit of those American pioneers and their love of freedom and sympathy for the under dog. With someone's liberty at stake, it was not possible for many of those newly arrived colonists to remain impassive. Companies of volunteers were formed north of the Rio Grande, and their commanders led them down into Mexico to fight by the sides of the Mexican patriots.

In the light of subsequent events, this display of patriotism proved to be a valuable experience for those first fighting men of Texas. It not only gave them needed military training, but also provided an insight into the character and tactics of the Mexican soldier which was of valuable help when they later waged their own war for independence. This association and contact also furnished those future American cowboys, who were to perfect the art of handling cattle to its highest degree, a chance to study and learn the fundamentals of stock raising at first hand, by observing the Mexican ranchers and their methods.

There was only a short breathing spell following the Mexican war for independence before the Texans started their own rebellion. The news of this conflict brought another movement of English-speaking people into the province. Many a young man in the states as far east as the Atlantic seaboard heard the battle cry and injected himself into the fray at the side of his embattled racial kin. For six long and bitter years those ragged and poorly armed patriots battled the hordes of invading Mexican soldiers on their front while the warring Indians charged down upon them from behind. The Mexican forces which had previously garrisoned the string of Spanish forts and missions across the country withdrew to join their own army, leaving the entire frontier unprotected.

After independence was gained the young Republic raised her head above the turmoil and staggered onward. She was weak to the point of exhaustion, and bleeding from her wounds, but there was no stopping. She was split by internal strife and dissension, but her leaders had stood through too much adversity to give way to despondency now. Most of those from the United States who had answered the battle call elected to remain in this land of great promise and freedom. Some secured land grants and built homes and settled down. Others remained to join the group of fighting men and wage war against the marauding Indians who had run wild and free from restraint during those fearful years when the life and liberty of all English-speaking people in the province hung in a balance. Now that their freedom was won, the Texans girded themselves for another conflict to meet the supreme test of courage.

The Texans had learned much about tactics as displayed in organized warfare from their battle experience with the Mexicans, but the brand of Indian warfare that they now faced was a new one. As stated formerly, the Indians in the country where the first settlements were formed were peacefully inclined and never engaged in hostilities. But now, the ones the white men rode out to meet in battle were of an entirely different class, and they were much harder to conquer than their late Mexican foes. Mounted on their swift horses, those savage fighters struck with the speed of lightning and the deadliness of a rattlesnake. From high up on the prairies, they came in large bands to kill and steal and then to fade away back into the hills like so many phantoms. They could pounce upon a lonely ranch or isolated settlement and murder the citizens and burn the houses in a matter of a few minutes and then retreat into the wilderness, driving all mobile livestock before them.

The men who headed the newly formed government were fully aware of the handicaps presented by the brand of warfare they were facing. Previous to this period, the major forces of opposing armies had been men on foot, with horsemen playing only a minor part. Even the battle of San Jacinto was won by infantrymen, and all Indian wars east of the Mississippi had been fought by foot men. But the Indians which now harassed the young Republic did not fight an organized warfare, nor did they seek a decisive battle. They appeared in great howling mobs at the break of dawn, and struck, and ran away. It was useless to attempt pursuit on foot. The government came to realize that their only hope of defending the country against the devastating raids and coping with the situation was to create a force of warriors just as mobile as, and more daring than, the foe. Thus, there came into being one of the most colorful bodies of fighting men the world has ever known — the Texas Rangers.

But the creation of a mounted fighting force did not solve the problem. Regardless of the white men's personal bravery and daring, and their knowledge of organized warfare, they were still at a serious disadvantage. They fought only with guns, except for a few, who armed themselves with sabers, while the Indians were skillful experts in the use of bows and arrows and lances.

The Texans had developed into good horsemen, but they were not as good as the Indians. Since the Indians fought only on horseback, in running battles, the Rangers still had to learn the art. In arms the Indians had them greatly outclassed. A Ranger could carry no more than two pistols and possibly one rifle and a saber, but his guns were good for only one shot each in a single clash. They were the old style muzzle-loader, single-shot,

cap-and-ball weapons, and it was impossible to measure powder and tamp a bullet into the barrel and fit a cap to the firing
chamber in battle while riding at high speed in the wind. The
old style rifle with its long barrel had been made solely for use by
a man who walked, and it turned out to be extremely unwieldy
and awkward to carry on horseback. Eventually the Rangers
discarded it and came to rely altogether on their pistols. Those
who attempted to fight with sabers found themselves greatly outclassed when they met the Indian lancers.

The latter were not only expert in the use of these weapons,
but their superior horsemanship and their perfectly trained
mounts gave them every advantage in tactics. An Indian could
flash in and out among another group of horsemen and do his
deadly work with a lance before his antagonist could get into
position to bring a saber to bear.

For two hundred years the Indians had been practicing their
own brand of warfare and training their horses exclusively for
that purpose. When there were no white men to fight, the inter-
tribal conflicts kept them at a fine point of condition and training. The Comanches and Apaches were traditional enemies, but
they now united against the white men, who were considered
to be the common foe. Each warrior had the pick of many animals for his war horses and he selected and trained the ones best
suited for his needs. They were trained so perfectly to perform
in a running battle that they required little more guiding than
the pressure of the rider's knee against one side or the other. A
rawhide string tied around under the jaw served as a bridle, but
it was seldom ever needed. His saddle consisted only of a small
piece of buffalo hide, with a strip of rawhide serving as a girth.
The Comanche was small in stature and his horses were never
burdened with needless weight. Those horses were endowed with
a strong constitution, and they could travel far and fast, either
carrying their riders into battle or fleeing to safety after a devastating raid.

If a Ranger's scope of effective fighting was limited to the number of loads he had in one or more of his guns, such was not the case with the Indians. Their supply of ammunition consisted of as many arrows as they could crowd into a slender rawhide quiver. They could reload by the simple operation of fitting another arrow to the bowstring. The only course open to a Ranger was to inflict as much damage as he could with the limited number of shots in his guns and then flee for safety. It went against the grain to run away from any kind of foe, but under the prevailing conditions they had no choice. It would have been rank suicide to make a stand long enough to reload their weapons.

The Indians carried a supply of arrows in a rawhide quiver slung across their backs, and lances were slipped through a loop at the waist, with the blunt end resting in a small rawhide boot fastened around an ankle. They shortened their bows to make them easy to manipulate on horseback, and they carried them loose in their hands. Upon one arm was a small shield made of buffalo hide when green, with two layers stitched together with thongs and then shaped and hardened. A strip of pliable and tanned rawhide inside the shield served as a handle to hold it secure. It was of such toughness that it would turn a saber thrust or deflect a bullet, except a direct and center shot. This completed the Comanche's war equipment. He carried no food, because he was able to sustain himself off the land wherever he traveled, and besides, he exercised little taste in its selection. A prairie dog, or even a snake, was not distasteful to him. All of an Indian's paraphernalia taken together weighed little more than a Ranger's two guns and lead bullets, to say nothing of his boots, spurs and saddle. When on the warpath, the Comanche was a formidable foe. He fought a hit-and-run brand of warfare that was entirely new to white men, and he forced them to fight his way.

Not only were the Rangers at a disadvantage in the class of weapons they used, but they were also greatly outclassed in horsemanship. Men who fought the Comanche Indian were unanimous in their agreement that he was the most expert horseman of all time. He was so proficient that he could cling to the side of a running horse, using the animal as a breastwork, and shoot arrows with deadly skill. With one leg thrown across the animal's back, and with heel digging into the sink in front of the hip bone, he stretched full length on the side away from danger and clung there with the point of his elbow hooked over the horse's withers, meanwhile dashing in circles around his prey. With his body thus protected, and nothing more than an arm and leg exposed, he made a very small and difficult target indeed. He could shoot his arrows from above or beneath the horse's neck. This was the situation the Rangers faced when they set out to drive the Indians from the frontier of Texas in 1836.

Coming in a slow and roundabout way by word of mouth from person to person, news of a new gun invention trickled down to those hard-pressed fighting men of the frontier. In 1837 they heard that a man by the name of Samuel Colt had made a pistol that would shoot six times without having to be reloaded. Both this man and his wonderful gun were in faraway New Jersey, in the United States, which to the Rangers might as well have been in another world. Even though the chances of securing such a gun were very remote, its alluring possibilities came in for much wishful speculation and discussion around the Ranger campfires. At last the Rangers were able to get certain officials of the Republic interested, but the result of inquiries sent out to responsible army men in the United States was not at all encouraging. It was learned from authentic sources that both the United States and the French war departments had tested the new gun and that both had rejected it as being impracticable and unreliable. Because of this failure to interest some government in the gun and secure orders for its manufacture, so the story went, the inventor had failed in business and had been forced into bankruptcy. His factory was closed down and all assets were in custody of the court, awaiting sale to satisfy his creditors' claims.

But the need of this gun was great, and the thought of bringing such a weapon to bear against the Indians was very intriguing. In spite of the adverse reports, the matter was touched upon more than once during discussions between the commander of the Ranger forces and the president of the Republic. It was common knowledge that the frontier was in grave danger and that nothing short of a miracle would save it. It was a far-fetched idea to send an emissary all the way to New Jersey for direct and first-hand information, but that was the only way to find out for certain. The situation was desperate, and the prospects of the advantage to be gained in warfare by securing such a gun were worth the expenditure of the necessary time and money to give it a fair test. Thus, staking a great deal upon a slim hope, a representative of the Ranger force was finally started upon the long journey to faraway New Jersey to see and talk with Samuel Colt and test the gun. He traveled overland on horseback to a Gulf port town and thence by the slow and tedious method of sailing ship to New York.

The Ranger succeeded in locating Samuel Colt, but he found conditions worse even than had been reported. It was true that the inventor had failed in business and that the small factory was closed down under lock of the bankruptcy referee. Colt had utterly abandoned the project, and he did not have in his possession, nor did he know where he could lay hands on, one of the guns to show his customer. Word brought by the Ranger revived his hopes, however, and after a lengthy search, he succeeded in finding a gun for the prospective buyer to test, and also to serve as a model for making others in case it won approval.

The gun that Colt produced was far from perfect, but it was superior to any of its kind the Ranger had ever seen. Its most valuable quality was that it could surely shoot six times without having to be reloaded. It still had to be charged with powder and ball by hand, and a cap had to be fitted to the firing tube, but the thought of six shots coming one after the other seemed like an answer to their prayer.

After making suggestions for changes in the structure of the gun and trying out the new model, the Ranger took the responsibility upon himself to order two thousand of them, to be manufactured and delivered within the earliest possible time. He then hastened back to Texas to relay the glad tidings and revive the hopes of his hard-pressed comrades.

With the newly executed contract of purchase in his possession to show his creditors, Colt was able to persuade them to withdraw the bankruptcy proceeding and release his factory from the court. From that time onward, it can be said that Samuel Colt was never again in financial difficulties. The transaction turned out to be of incalculable benefit to both parties. It has been truly said that Colt saved the Republic of Texas — but Texas also saved Colt. It was only a short time after the initial order had been filled before the Colt six-shooter became indispensable all over the Western Hemisphere.

The new gun that the returning Ranger exhibited to his comrades embodied the main principles of the modern revolver. It had a cylinder of six chambers that revolved on a spindle from a dog set in the lower part of the hammer, which moved upward each time the hammer was cocked. Its most noteworthy feature was that the cylinder harbored six sure-fire shots that could be discharged one after another without reloading. The Rangers were keenly impatient for a chance to try it against their perennial foe.

The Indians had long ago learned the fallacy of the white man's weapons. They knew that a Ranger seldom ever carried more than two pistols and that these were good for only one shot each. It had been their strategy to draw the Rangers' fire and then force them into a running fight. It was a stunning and costly surprise to the Indians when they met twelve withering blasts of gunfire from each Ranger instead of only the two they had expected.

Other and better guns were to follow. The greatest contribution to long distance shooting, and second only to the six-shooter, was made when Oliver Winchester came out with his repeating rifle. The Winchester rifle was made with a short barrel and was especially designed for carrying and firing on horseback. It was light of weight and could be manipulated as easily as the Indians handled their bows and arrows. Its greatest advantage was the metallic cartridge, which did away with the necessity of measuring powder and tamping it into the barrel. It had a magazine that held six cartridges, and a loaded shell could be thrown into the barrel by the simple operation of working a lever back and forth. The adoption and employment of the Winchester rifle was so universal throughout the West that the name became synonymous with rifles. While Colt's revolver came generally to be known as the six-shooter, many men rode the ranges who thought of the word Winchester only as a rifle, and not as the inventor's name.

It is claimed by some authorities that the repeating rifle had more to do with beating the Indians into subjugation than any other single element. It was not only an important weapon to be used against them in battle, but it was also instrumental in destroying the buffalo, which was their main food supply. Buffalo hunters made inroads upon the vast herds with the single-shot rifle, but this was nothing compared to the destruction that was wrought when the repeating rifle was adopted. Thus, with their food supply destroyed, the Indians were forced to desist in their warfare and to retreat to their reservations, where they became wards of the Government.

While the Indians eventually came into possession of all modern guns and discarded their bows and arrows in favor of them, they never regained the advantage they once held when they fought with bows and arrows and the white men fought with guns that were good for only a single shot at a time. White people were now spreading to all regions west of the Mississippi and carrying on an unrelenting war against them. It can be truly said that from the day the first Ranger strapped a six-shooter to his belt and the first frontiersman laid a repeating rifle across his saddle bow, the Plains Indians were on the road to destruction.

When the first band of Rangers rode out with their new six-shooters, the Indians might just as well have started their death song. The Indian wars in the prairie country were to last for many years to come, but there was never a question as to the ultimate result of the conflict. Although greatly outnumbered and out-mounted, the Rangers slowly but surely waged a winning war, as they gradually pushed the Indians back and back to make room for the booming cattle industry that was ready to dawn.

CHAPTER THREE

THE COWBOY
FINDS HIS ROPE

Dᴜʀɪɴɢ the period between Texas' Independence and its annexation to the United States, a great expansion had been under way. The Republic rewarded with land grants all who took part in the war for independence, and held out inducements to any newcomer who cared to cast his lot among the people of this new nation. The Rangers had been successful in pushing the Indians farther back into the interior, thereby expanding the frontier, and close behind them was an ever present wave of adventurous pioneers.

A sizable number of the inhabitants were beginning to reflect upon the possibilities offered by ranching. The cattle brought into the country were showing a remarkable increase in number, and were mixing more or less with the wild Spanish stock. Up to this time the American farmer in Texas had regarded the cattle end of his business merely as a side line in the scheme of living. The only salable animals among the increase were fully grown steers, fattened for slaughter at the local meat markets, or matured oxen for draft purposes.

Although there was little prospect of markets in sight, those men who were determined to build an empire out of the raw wilderness and who had backed up that determination with their guns and their lives, could see in the dim and distant future a chance for the industry. They reasoned that many people on the continent were in need of the cheap beef that could be produced in this raw country, and that eventually a means would be formulated to bring them together. Down along the Rio Grande border and in the lower Gulf Coast regions, the Mexicans who had successfully held onto their ranches were fairly well along with the undertaking of raising cattle. With reference to markets, they were somewhat better situated than the English-speaking colonists farther north and east. There was some demand for beef on the hoof in the interior of Mexico. A number of cattle were driven overland to these markets, while a few ships capable of transporting live animals occasionally took on a cargo at ports around the mouth of the Rio Grande. Although the Mexicans were the first to engage actively in the cattle business, they never increased their operations to a large scale until the possibilities were demonstrated by the Americans.

As the English-speaking settler began to feel his way into the new venture, some vexatious problems arose. His heretofore small herd of animals was gentle and easily kept under restraint, but as the herd increased in numbers, the animals were inclined to stray into the open and unfenced ranges. Now and then, one would drift away from home, mix with the wild cattle of the prairies and grow entirely out of the owner's knowledge. Some men devised means of marking their animals so that they would be recognizable among others, such as sawing off one horn or cutting slits in one or both ears, etc., etc. But this practice proved to be unsatisfactory. Too many men employed the same methods. Before long, this fact caused more or less confusion, and numerous disputes of ownership resulted. Although the animals in question represented little monetary value, there was something about the early pioneers that made them want what was theirs, and they were determined to have it.

In time, those future cattle barons, who were groping blindly at their new calling, took a cue from the Mexican ranchers and started branding their animals. Long ago, the Mexicans had evolved the method of marking their range animals by branding them with a hot iron. The practice was said to have been started by a Spaniard whose Indian slaves were so numerous that he employed this means of identifying them. Nevertheless, the practice was in use by the Mexicans long before any American took it up. By its adoption, a wide and unlimited range of identification marks was brought into use. Many ingenious and novel symbols and combinations were created — the Square and Compass, the Ace of Clubs, the Deuce of Hearts, the Spade, the Spur, for example.

In later years, when cow thieves became prevalent and preyed upon stockmen, the cattle raiser strove to select a symbol, or letter, or a combination of them, that could not be made into some other brand — such as running a *P* into an *R,* or a *T* into a cross, to mention some of the simpler examples. Thus, with his brand established upon his own cattle and recognized by his neighbors, the pioneer settler in the wild country assumed more poise and bearing as he became a man of property. He could now look forward to an income from another source than digging it out of the soil by hard and drudging labor.

As the Indians had learned to catch and tame the wild horses runnning loose upon the range, so did the Texans. The trade of saddle making quickly spread, and the artisans found an unlimited demand for their product. There were no tanneries to treat and cure saddle leather in the country, but experiments proved that tanned leather was not indispensable to saddle making. These newly created cowmen learned from the Indians and Mexicans that dressed rawhide, cured by hand-working, and oiled with fats from the same animals that had produced the hide, was a usable, and first-rate substitute for tanned leather.

The one scarcity that seemed at first to have no substitute was that of saddle trees. They were the work of a craftsman, and there were few of them in the business. However, it has truly been said that the enormity of the need will supply the means, and such was the case in this instance. There were a number of woodworkers in the country, such as wagon and cart repairmen, timber dressers and log-house builders. Many a blacksmith and carpenter forsook his trade and embarked upon the more lucrative career of saddle-tree maker with his woodworking tools. The demand for saddles had become so great that the tree-makers did not have to bother about covering the new products of their craftsmanship. They found a ready sale for all naked trees they were able to turn out, and they left it up to their customers to cover the tree and rig the saddle as their fancy suited.

After annexation of the Republic, the colonists were provided with still more room for expansion. The United States Government erected a string of forts from east to west which, roughly speaking, brought the southern half of the state within its protective zone.

As part of the annexation agreements, the Government had contracted to remove all Indians from the state and quarter them upon their reservations elsewhere. This did not compel the Indians to keep their end of the bargain by any means. In spite of the agreement, and the United States Army to back it up, the Indians still carried on their hit-and-run warfare. The string of forts did not bring protection to those within the zone. The outposts were far apart, and inadequately manned. The Comanches still slipped through the lines, and conducted their devastating raids. They pillaged and burned, and stole horses, and in later years when the supply of buffalo had dwindled, they drove herds of cattle ahead of them as they retreated to the sanctuary of the High Plains country or to their reservations in the present states of Oklahoma and New Mexico.

The war between the United States and Mexico was not without its benefit to the youngest state within the Union. Although many of her native sons attached themselves one way or another to the United States Army and died upon the battlefields, the presence of that great army along the southern border of the state furnished ample protection for that area. This served to release many fighting men who had been quartered in the zone, to resume the fight with the Indians from the High Plains. The war was also an incentive to the cattle business. The vast troops needed meat supplies, and many surplus cattle were disposed of by selling them to the Army for food.

By the end of this war, the cattle country of Texas was suffering with growing pains. Cattle on the range were increasing in such prodigious numbers that it seemed as though the state would burst from the expansion. There is no basis for computation of the number at that time, but it was almost beyond comprehension. It is said that in later years, when the trade was booming, a rancher newly engaged in the business wanted a quick estimate of prospects for a huge profit. He enlisted the services of a biologist to make the calculation for him. This learned gentleman figured that, under normal conditions, one hundred head of mother cows would increase to the unbelievable number of fourteen hundred head in ten years. These figures are no doubt greatly exaggerated by the rancher's wishful thinking, but even so, by using the above formula as a basis for calculating the number of cattle in Texas, the result would be staggering. If the Spaniards lost only one hundred head during their first invasions, and if the biologist's estimated rate of increase were cut in half, and if a generous allowance were made for Indian consumption and wild animal destruction, the result would still be unbelievable after two hundred years of propagation.

By 1850, a few men were bunching small numbers of cattle together with the view of making the growth of livestock their main calling. With this development, the cattle business entered into its first phase. A limited market for aged steers fit for butchering had grown up in New Orleans and other Mississippi River towns. With this faint breath of life being transmitted into the infant industry, more or less trading and bartering were in evidence. For the first time in the history of Texas, the cattle speculator appeared upon the scene. Many of these individuals were gentry of shady repute, whose characters would not stand too close an inspection, but nevertheless, they injected themselves into the trade by buying up small bunches of cattle for the markets. In some instances they drove them themselves, but in others, they contracted for delivery at the Mississippi, where they were ferried across the river.

These drives offered few or no problems, and they could not be compared with the real trail herds that were to come later. They were made through a region that was fairly well settled, and free of the Indian menace. Since the few herds were made up of gentle animals in small bunches, their handling required little or no skill.

Now, with this incentive to spur them on, the owners of breeding herds pushed farther back onto the frontier where range was fresh and grass more plentiful. They erected crude cabins of native logs or stone near the best watering places, and waited for the next year's crop of marketable steers to mature. For the most part these first small bunches of cattle were gentle and were kept constantly under herd. This was to prevent them from straying away and mixing with wild animals of the regions, and also as a protective measure against theft by Indians. Those early cattlemen had not yet learned the rough-riding tactics and skillful rope-throwing prowess of their followers, who were never daunted by the prospect of having to recover a straying animal from its hideout in the brush thickets and canyon bottoms. Thus, either the owner or his hired man, or his partner, was constantly with the first herds.

In the beginning, all ranchmen made a practice of penning their cattle at night. Corrals made of poles or rock fences to hold them were erected close to the ranch houses. Later, ranchmen learned that when cattle were well located upon ample feed and water, and remained unmolested, they had little or no incentive to drift away during a single night. It was also learned that the animals thrived much better when not under constant restraint. The vigilance was gradually relaxed by leaving them alone at night, but they were kept under observation during the day in a loose herding sort of arrangement. From that, they were left alone during the daytime, and kept under control by a still looser lineriding operation, which prevented them from straying completely out of bounds. By the end of 1850, many future ranchmen and cattle barons were scattered over the prairies of Central Texas and deep into the south-central part of the state.

In some cases two young men not encumbered by family responsibilities formed a partnership for the venture. It was to be many years before it was safe for women and children out on the frontier where cattle thrived the best. Although some braved the dangers, many lost their lives from the venture. But the partnership arrangement seemed to have been the most satisfactory and practical. A single man had only himself and his own safety to look after, and by two of them being together, they furnished company and protection for one another. When it was necessary to make the long and arduous journey to town for needed supplies or other business transactions, one of the partners made the trip alone while the other stayed and kept watch on the stock. Thus, one man was always in attendance with the cattle. Charles Goodnight, who was the premier of all cattlemen and who did more towards developing the industry than any other one man, started out in this manner. Many of those associations established a friendship that lasted down through the years and was only broken by the death of one party or the other. It was a rarity that a partnership was ever dissolved through dissension or misunderstandings. The law of give and take ruled absolute, and tolerance and self-sacrifice were the main elements of everyday life.

The life of those early-day ranchers was not one of ease and comfort, by any means. It was a lonely existence, to say the least, and it was beset by many dangers. Indians were always on the prowl, and next to a white man's horses, his scalp was the most coveted prize. Because of the large area needed for grazing purposes, the ranches were of necessity long distances apart. This did not amount to much of an inconvenience at that time. The ranchers had accumulated horses and were breeding more, and they were learning how to ride to the best advantage. There was more or less contact and association between those widely separated pioneers. They often helped each other out with any work that could not be well attended to alone, such as the erection of a new structure, or the seasonal branding. During an Indian raid the alarm would be spread to the various ranches by one or more messengers mounted upon a fast horse, and they all rallied for a stand against their traditional foe.

During slack times they went on cow-hunting expeditions. Many wild cattle still inhabited inaccessible areas, and they belonged to anyone who could get his brand upon their hides.

Any captured animals not only made valued additions to a man's holdings, but the sport of catching them was also most thrilling. While the trips into the haven of the wild bunches were far from the well-organized and smooth-running outfits that were to come later, they might well be called the first roundups. So wide was the scope of operation and so general was the practice by all ranchmen that cow hunting became an institution and a by-word. There are still a few men living who refer to any kind of a roundup as a cow hunt.

A group of neighbors would assemble at a given point. They would pack one or more horses with necessary provisions and a scant supply of blankets for bedding and would take along an extra saddle horse for a change of mounts in case of emergency. They drove before them a small bunch of gentle cattle to serve as decoys, and with them would be a few work oxen to be used as snubbers if needed. They timed their arrival at the scene of operations a short while before sundown. This was planned in order to give them a chance to look over the terrain before darkness, and still not expose their presence more than necessary to the wild cattle. They endeavored to pitch camp at the dividing line between open spots of prairie and the heavy brush of the creek bottoms where the wild ones lay in hiding during the day. When camp was made, horses would be hobbled or staked out, and the small bunch of decoys held closely under herd during the night.

If allowed to pursue their natural instincts and habits, no cow animal will remain in heavy brush during a spring or summer night when prairie is accessible. The weather is cooler, the grazing is better, and the onslaughts of mosquitoes and other nocturnal pests are less severe in the open than in the lowlands. While waiting for the appropriate hour to spring their trap, the hunters were careful to make as little noise as possible.

Before the first streaks of dawn lined the sky, the cowmen would be in their saddles. The bunch of decoy cattle would be pushed gently toward the open prairie and released. Having been driven the day before and held closely together during the night without a chance to feed, the hungry animals would spread out and drift away from their place of confinement while they eagerly tried to satisfy their appetites. In doing so, they would mix more or less with their wild neighbors. The horsemen would skirt around the edge of the brush where it met with the prairie and endeavor to place themselves at strategic points between the prey and their hideouts. They would then begin slowly to round up the wild and the gentle cattle together.

When the wild animals discovered that they were being hemmed in by men on horseback, they invariably made a dash for liberty. It was then that the fast riding took place, while the horsemen tried to hold them in a bunch with the decoys. If the hunters were lucky, they gathered from ten to fifty head, but sometimes they gathered none at all. No matter how well the movement was planned and executed, some of the wildest ones would breach the line and break away from the hard-riding men. If a man failed to turn one back into the bunch, he would take down his rope and endeavor to catch it before it reached the brush haven. It was seldom that a roper had a chance to make more than one throw, and it had be a good one. If the catch succeeded, he would throw his victim to the ground and tie its feet together. One of the gentle oxen would be brought up and the two would be necked together and then turned loose. As certain as day followed night, that work ox would bring the obstreperous wild animal into the home ranch in the course of a day or two.

The herd would then be driven to a strong corral where the wild ones were earmarked and branded. An equal division of the spoils would be made between those who took part in the hunt. After several days of herding with gentle cattle on the ranch, the wild ones usually reconciled themselves to the situation and settled down in their new location. If one or more did escape and return back to the rough and brushy country, it made little difference. The owner's brand was upon its hide, a mark which could never be erased. Those first range cowmen were fast learning to be experts with their ropes, and a wild cow loose in the brush or rough country created little or no problem for them.

By the time those future cowmen were venturing out upon their first cow hunts, ropes, as we know them today, were fairly well developed. The Mexicans had been using them for many years. It is not known just when they were first employed, but certainly the art of roping belongs to the New World. Ropes had never before been used as instruments for ensnaring loose animals until comparatively recent times. This cow-and horse-catching rope was first known as *la reata,* which is Spanish for the rope, and it supports the belief that the Mexicans were the first to employ its use in such a manner. The words were later contracted into one — lariat.

The first lariats were made of horsehair spun into long strands and then twisted tightly together. These were far better than none at all, but they did not serve their purpose nearly so well as others that were introduced later on. They lacked sufficient weight to carry against the wind when thrown from the back of a running horse, and after a certain amount of use, the twists had a tendency to loosen up, and the strands pull apart. Following the hair rope, the rawhide *reata* was evolved, and it remained in general use up to the turn of the century. Indeed, these *reatas* were so popular that many men clung to them as late as the 1920's.

The first rawhide ropes were crudely made and consisted of two strands of hide twisted together. The knack of cutting an entire hide into a single strand and braiding it had not been learned, and the products of those first rope makers were clumsy and unwieldy affairs indeed. Finally, a third strand was added to the twist. This was some improvement, but later when the art of braiding was put into practice, the rope was brought almost to a state of perfection. Four, six, and sometimes twelve strands of uniform size were braided together. When properly cured, oiled with animal fat, and occasionally drenched in fresh blood, the rawhide rope was a very satisfactory and necessary part of a cowboy's equipment.

This rope had the correct weight and balance for throwing against the wind. It was resilient and pliable, and when in the hands of an expert, the loop would sail beautifully and unerringly over the horns of an animal running far ahead of the roper. The standard length of a rope is thirty-three feet, but so proficient did some of the Mexican and California vaqueros become with the rawhide *reatas* that they often used them forty, and in some rare instances fifty, feet long.

The only objection to the rawhide *reata* was that its structure was of such a nature that it would not stand a sudden shock. It had sufficient strength when the strain was brought against it gradually, but a quick snap often resulted in breaking one or more strands. After that, it was useless as a catching rope. To prevent such an occurrence, the practice of throwing a coil around the saddle horn and letting a little slack run as the strain came on was evolved. This was the basis for the famous phrase of *"da le vuelta"* which became a part of a cowboy's speech and was in general use up to the end of the century. The term became almost a by-word, being universal over the cattle country, and could be heard time and again at a roundup, or upon the branding ground, or at any other place where roping was done. It is doubtful if one out of fifty cowboys employed upon the ranches at this time understands its implication.

The expression is purely Spanish and was coined by the Mexican vaqueros. Like many other Spanish words and phrases, it was soon adopted by the American cowboy. It means simply "give it a turn," but the simplicity of the meaning in no way detracted from its popularity. Some Americans corrupted the term by running it into two words and by mispronunciation. Writers have butchered it further in both misspelling and incorrect translation. Some refer to the term as "dalle welte," "dally weltee," and there is at least one gross violation on record where an author called it "dolly welty."

Thus, in order to keep his rawhide *reata* from breaking, the American cowboy learned to employ the *da le vuelta*. Instead of having the end tied securely to the saddle horn, he would simply "give it a turn" and let some slack run out as the strain came against it. The operation was intricate to perform and required extreme dexterity and quickness to complete successfully. Many a novice or clumsy-fingered man has had one or more fingers pinched off by getting them caught between the rope and the saddle horn.

In later years better ropes took the place of the *reata*. They could be bought in the open market, where formerly the user of a rawhide rope had to make it himself or find some person who could be persuaded to make it for him. The rawhide *reatas* were never a generally marketed product. The new fibre ropes that were developed proved to be just as lively and just as pliable and much stronger than those made of either hair or rawhide. The art of lariat making has reached a state of near perfection, and the experts performing in the rodeos today can ask for nothing better.

CHAPTER FOUR

THE HERDS
BEGIN TO MOVE

DURING the period between 1850 and the outbreak of the War Between the States, there was increasing activity in the cattle business. The ranch herds were growing in size, and new markets were opening up to the trade. Texas cattle were finding their way to the Eastern States by overland routes and by sea.

Ships called at ports along the Gulf Coast for a limited number of cattle, and a well-defined trail, designated as the Opalousas Route, was laid out into Louisiana. The first packing plant in the country was erected at one of the port towns and a considerable number of cattle were slaughtered for export. There was not adequate refrigeration available to preserve fresh beef, so it was put through a pickling process of curing. This was done by forcing salt brine into the meat under heavy pressure. As a preservative measure, the operation was successful, but it did not add flavor to the product. The plant remained in operation for the duration of the war, but it failed when the great trails were opened up. The meat-eating population of the country showed a preference for beef fresh off the block to that cured by impregnation with salt brine.

While the packing plant was in operation on the Gulf Coast, and a considerable number of cattle were being driven to the Mississippi over the Opalousas Route, some cowmen were feeling their way in other directions. At least two enterprising drovers succeeded in taking their herds to Peoria, Illinois. There is a story of one going to western Pennsylvania. However, this seems to be more of a legend than a historical fact. No one knew the parties and no recording of the event was made. The owners never returned, and no one ever heard of them after they were supposed to have crossed the Texas border. Be that as it may, there was beyond question a firm demand in the North and East for Texas beef, and drovers found a ready sale waiting upon delivery.

The country where the first herds originated among the English-speaking people of the state was not best adapted for growing cattle. As stated previously, the location was selected for farming purposes and not cattle raising. Neither was the land which the first routes traversed suitable for driving large herds. There were great areas of timber and swamp, and numerous rivers, and the cattle drives were made under serious difficulties. Nor were they without their tragedies. One of the early drovers,

who traveled the Opalousas Route, was drowned while swim-
ming a river, and his two sons abandoned the herd in order to
take his body back home for burial. They then returned, gathered
the cattle and continued on to their destination. Those first herds
consisted of gentle animals, and they were of necessity in small
bunches. The nature of the country, and climate, coupled with
the inexperience of the drovers, prohibited handling large numbers of cattle in one herd.

During the War Between the States, the herds increased in
both size and volume. Many cattle were driven East to feed the
Confederate armies. Gradually, the cattlemen mastered the art
of handling large numbers in a single herd, and they also learned
to stick to the high grounds and prairies with them when it was
possible to do so.

It is during this period that the name of John Chisum first
appears upon the pages of cattle history. This man was to become
the largest rancher the world had known up to his time, and he
was one of the first to sense the advantage of ranching on the
prairies instead of in the timber. During the war, Chisum grew
into a full-fledged trail man, as he drove hundreds and hundreds
of cattle through to the Mississippi for the Confederate Army. At
the close of the war he moved his holding out onto the frontier
when there was little or no protection from the Indians except
what he could effect himself. He surrounded himself with a class
of fighting cowboys who feared nothing the Indians had to offer;
and while waiting for reconstruction to run its course, he protected his property by sheer courage and force of guns.

At this time, the cattle business in Texas received a damag-
ing setback. Outside of the few who secured contracts from the
Confederate Government to furnish beef for the armies, a stale-
mate settled upon the growers. They were cut off from any other
market and practically all those young men who had braved the
Indian frontier to engage in the business dropped things as they
were and went to war. With the beginning of hostilities between

the two sections, all attempts of the Federal Government to keep the Indian tribes that bordered upon the Southern states upon their reservations were discontinued. In fact, the Government reversed its former policy. Northern sympathizers and agents worked among the tribes, stirring up old hatreds and inciting them to new atrocities. Once more, while the fighting men of Texas were facing one foe, the warring Indians swept down from distant hideouts through the back door. In this manner, many able-bodied men were tied down at home to protect the scattered settlements against their old perennial foes. Indians were no respecters of persons, and a woman's or a child's scalp was coveted just as much as that of a man.

Ranches on the frontier were abandoned, and families were moved into settlements for safety. Nearly every man able to ride a horse and fire a gun was either with the army up north, or with the Rangers fighting Indians. Protection of the settlements was left to the aged and cripples. The cattle that had been deserted grew up unattended and unbranded, and many of them reverted to their wild state. The Indians had learned the value of cow meat as a food, and they made away with many of these animals. They would have appropriated more, but they had not yet mastered the art of cow hunting, and the Rangers were making things too hot for them to waste much time in learning.

As in all wars, there were a few men too cowardly to fight, but greedy enough to fatten themselves at the expense of their more patriotic neighbors. Some of these slackers managed to start and maintain cattle herds of their own by branding calves belonging to those absent from home. It is fitting to say that the fruits of their greed and unpatriotic deeds did them little good. When they paused in their operations and looked about for a way to cash their ill-gotten gains, they found themselves to be hemmed in. The Confederate armies lay between them and possible outlet for their stolen chattels to the east, and the recently loosed, and desperate, Indian tribes dominated the plains to the north. They could well surmise the punishment that would be dished out to them when the ranchmen returned from war. Many desisted in their practices, and got out with their whole hides while getting was good.

It was a disheartened group of men who returned from losing a war to find their ranch houses burned and their personal belongings destroyed. Their cattle were scattered, and the increase was claimed by others. The Indians had driven away most of the horses the army had not requisitioned, and the returned soldiers found their ancient foe bolder, and more arrogant than ever. All the advantage gained by those years of desperate fighting had been lost and they were poorly equipped to renew the battles.

But those men who had fought Indians all their lives, and who had spent the last four years fighting their English-speaking cousins, were not the kind to sit in dejection and self-pity. As quickly as they could re-arm and re-mount themselves, punitive expeditions were carried out against the Indians. Their wrath was terrible and vengeance was swift. Before long the Comanches were reeling back to their hideouts and reservations. It is true that many devastating raids were made by the Indians in later years, but this was the last time they were able to make any kind of an organized stand.

Now, the ranchers turned their attention to rehabilitating themselves. They rebuilt their houses, and those with families re-established them in their homes. They rounded up their few remaining cattle and prepared to secure more. Many cattle roamed the range unclaimed and unbranded. Customs of the country and laws of the land decreed that these unbranded animals belonged to the man who could get his brand upon them first. Those rejuvenated cowmen rode high, wide, and handsome, early and late, and flung their ropes with skill and perseverance. The ones with the best horses and those the most proficient with their ropes, and the quickest with their branding irons, secured the largest additions to their herds.

With some of his former position established, the cowman found other obstacles in his path. He was entirely without money, and a long and hazardous distance separated him from prospective markets for his stock. There was a demand for cattle in the North and the money was there to pay for them, but a country infested by hostile Indians with whom he had been fighting for forty years lay in between. And how those destitute and hard-pressed Texans needed that money! The temptation was strong, and little time was lost in hesitation. Soon the herds were moving.

In order to eliminate the risk of encountering hostile Indians, the first drives swung eastward into Arkansas and through the Ozarks to the railroad at Sedalia, Missouri. This route would not have been out of line had the herds been small ones and had they consisted of gentle stock as in former years. Such was not the case at this time. During the war, the practice of handling large numbers of cattle had been developed, and most animals had grown wild running loose upon the range. The attempts to move prairie cattle through a mountainous and brushy country were dogged by misfortune, and the fallacy of such an undertaking was soon apparent.

The herds of Longhorns passing through the Ozarks stampeded at the least provocation and scattered among the mountains like so many rabbits. Valuable time was lost and heartbreaking work was required to bunch them together; and by then they were ready for another stampede. The animals' feet developed softness from walking through the water-soaked valleys, and the sharp rocks of the hills cut them into shreds. They would not feed upon the coarse grass of the region, but partly satisfied their hunger on oak leaves and acorns, which shrunk them in flesh to almost skin and bones. There was a growing hostility among the farmers along the trail because of damage to their crops, and they had begun to suspect that the Texas Longhorns were responsible for numerous deaths among their own stock from a peculiar fever malady. After many costly failures, the futility of moving cattle in numbers over the Sedalia Route was acknowledged and the course abandoned.

But Texas was still raising cattle in large numbers and the state was still poverty-stricken. The sale of cattle was the only means of securing the needed money, and the only market for them was in the North. The people of Louisiana and other Southern states were just as destitute as the Texans, and there was no hope for relief in that direction. Another route had to be established, and a compromise on a middle course between the warring Indians on one side and the mountains on the other was finally settled upon.

The so-called Five Civilized Indian Tribes were quartered upon the eastern part of the Indian Territory. This area was partly prairie and partly timber, with a percentage of rough land, but was much more desirable for a cattle trail than the Ozark country. There was some speculation as to the attitude the Indians would take when the herds began to move, but the only way to know for certain was to try it and find out. The first herds met with no objection, but as they increased in volume, and when the Indians saw their own grazing range swept bare by the thousands and thousands of Longhorns trailing across it, they lodged strong protests. They demanded and collected a heavy tribute for each herd passing through. At first they were satisfied to take cattle in payment, but when their own stock became afflicted with that peculiar fever which had broken out among the Missouri farm cattle, they were satisfied with nothing short of money paid in hand. To prevent spreading of the malady, they designated a certain route for the herds to follow, and they saw that the cattle were held within the bounds whether there was grass for them to eat or not.

The route through the Indian Nations led to Baxter Springs, Kansas, in the southeastern part of the state. The objections raised by the Indians were mild in comparison to what the drovers encountered when they attempted to cross the Kansas border.

It had been fairly well decided by this time that the fever which attacked cattle in the northern climes was transmitted to them by ticks that the Texas cattle carried into the country. Texas animals had become immune from the ravages since calfhood, but when one of the parasites sank its bill into the bloodstreams of a native Northern cow, the result was nearly always fatal. Now, whichever way a drover turned with his herd, he met a mob of armed and determined men threatening dire punishment for invasion of their provinces.

In the meantime, herds were piling up before the shipping point and market of Baxter Springs. Some drovers sought to circumvent the forbidden area by crossing over into Missouri and driving along the border between the two states to another outlet. Most of them found that they had jumped from the frying pan into the fire. Border ruffians who were residues of the Kansas bushwhacker and Missouri guerrilla bands of wartimes took advantage of the unsettled conditions and preyed upon the cowmen without mercy. Large numbers of cattle and large amounts of money were extracted from the unfortunate drovers under the threat of confiscation and destruction of their property. If one refused to pay the tribute, severe redress awaited him. His herd was stampeded, and many animals were killed and scattered through the hills. In some cases drovers were beaten and subjected to other outrages, and in other cases wanton murder was committed. Sharp-dealing and conscience-less bargainers were always in waiting, and many succeeded in buying the herds of cattle at prices ruinous for the cattlemen. It was estimated that two hundred thousand cattle were sacrificed in the Baxter Springs area in the year of 1866. It was a most discouraging experience for the men seeking an outlet for their cattle, but the desperate situation forced them to take the risks. Many a cowman cast wistful glances toward the High Plains of the Indian country, and a few decided to take their chances with their ancient foe.

By 1866, the United States Army had re-established the line of forts that extended from the Kansas border across the Indian Territory and Texas to the Rio Grande. While it was some consolation for the ranchers to know of the Army's presence, it was of little practical benefit. The Army then, as now, was bound more or less by red tape, and could not move fast enough in an emergency to keep pace with the Indians, who struck their blows and faded away like so many shadows. A story is told of an instance which may serve to illustrate the point.

It is said that a small body of Rangers attached themselves to a troop of cavalry for a joint pursuit against a large band of Indians that had raided the settlements, committed many murders, and driven away a large number of horses. The Rangers had worked ahead on the trail and were fast pulling away from the soldiers. The Ranger captain realized that his little band was so badly outnumbered by the Indians that they would have no chance against them. In desperation the Ranger rode back and approached the captain of the cavalry.

"Cain't you and yo'r men ride a little faster, Cap'n?" he urged.

"My orders are to proceed at a cautious and moderate pace until contact is made with the enemy," the Army man answered, irritated at a suggestion from the uneducated and uncouth Ranger.

"Do you shore 'nough want to make contact with them Injuns, Cap'n?" the Ranger asked.

"Certainly!" the cavalryman snapped.

"Wal," replied the Ranger philosophically, "you might meet them a-comin' back someday — but I swear you'll never ketch up with 'em."

While the Texans were chafing at idleness and trying to find a way around the barrier that separated them from the market for their cattle, another man was working to the same end. A cattle trader and promoter from Illinois, by name of Joseph McCoy, had long ago seen the great possibilities of the cattle trade, and he was trying to perfect a plan that would bring buyer and seller together. Like the Texans, he knew that cattle were in demand in the North, and he saw a chance to create a market on the raw prairie. Now events were shaping themselves to aid McCoy in his scheme.

The great railroad-building era was just getting started. The Kansas Pacific Company had extended its line westward to the edge of the Kansas prairie. They had hopes of building through to the Pacific Coast in the uncertain and distant future, but now the terminus rested far from the goal. Farms were too thick and farmers too hostile to cattlemen in the Topeka and Junction City areas for either place to serve as a cattle market.

McCoy reasoned correctly that it should be at a place devoid of trees, mountains or large streams and, by all means, away from farmers. After spending much time in talk, while painting a glowing picture of the cattle-trade possibilities, he succeeded in persuading the railroad men to extend the line a few miles farther west onto the wild and unsettled prairie. After much exploration and investigation, the little village and trading post of Abilene, Kansas, was selected for the cattle-shipping site. The town consisted of only one store and a saloon, but it was ideally situated for the purpose. There was plenty of water for large herds and there was an unlimited amount of grass right up to the edge of the little town. Neither were there any farmers in evidence.

Other than building the main line to the designated spot, and putting in a switch track for handling empty cars and a Wye for turning the engine, the railroad would go no farther. It was up to McCoy to erect the shipping pens; this he did in a grand manner. He knew it would take something strong and spacious to hold those great herds of Longhorns that he envisioned soon to be coming. The railroad was to pay him a stipulated amount for each car of cattle loaded. With the program of stockyard erection well under way, McCoy set about the task of swinging cattle to his shipping point. He secured a surveyor's compass to guide him and, with a camp outfit, staked a straight line from Abilene to the Indian Territory border. He marked the route by spading up blocks of prairie sod and building monuments high as a man's head to serve as a guide for the herds. With that out of the way, he mounted a horse and set out alone down through the Indian country toward Texas.

On his southward trip, McCoy encountered a well-defined trail that ran from the trading post of Wichita, Kansas, almost to the northern border of Texas at Red River. This trail had been laid out by the half-breed Indian trader, Jesse Chisholm. Chisholm was not a cowman by any means, and probably never owned more bovine stock than the oxen needed to pull his freight outfits. He never dreamed that he was creating a trail that was to be the greatest cattle highway the world had ever known. McCoy observed the lay of the land traversed by the Chisholm Trail and concluded that it would serve admirably as an extension of the route he had laid out through Kansas.

While McCoy was riding southward in search of someone with enough courage to brave the Indian country, one man was already on his way. He was Thompson, from down in the wild cattle country, and he had had his fill of the Ozark and Baxter Springs trails. His destination was uncertain, but he was determined to swing around the hostile farmers who lay between him and sale of his stock. He drove two thousand head of long-horned steers, and he had a crew of twenty men and a hundred saddle horses. At an unknown spot in the Indian country McCoy, the promoter, and Thompson, the trail driver, met face to face.

The best thing McCoy could do was talk. If he had not been so gifted, he would never have succeeded in persuading those doubting Kansas Pacific railroad officials to extend their line to Abilene on the prospect of the cattle trade. Now he brought to bear all his powers of argument upon Thompson, and he nearly overplayed his hand. The glowing accounts of the prospective market and shipping point were spread on so thick that Thompson grew skeptical, and McCoy almost lost his first customer.

Thompson was worldly wise, and he knew that McCoy was a Yankee. It had been only a short time since their kind had faced each other in mortal combat. Those were the first kind and encouraging words a Texan had ever heard spoken by a Northern man, and it was hard for Thompson to believe the good tidings. His experience with the Kansas bushwhackers had not served to abate his distrust. Thompson reflected over the proposition a long time before he was able to make up his mind. Before committing himself, he consulted with his men to search out their attitude, and pointed out the danger of being led into a trap. He stipulated that, in such an event, he intended to fight, and he wanted to sound out their willingness to stand and fight with him. When he was assured that they were willing to follow his leadership and fight by his side if necessary, the momentous decision was reached, and he passed his word to McCoy that he would drive to Abilene.

As though McCoy's charming personality had enchanted the entire region and brushed aside all obstacles, the venture was crowned with success. There has never been a cattle drive made with more ease and pleasure than this one was. Two thousand head of wild long-horned steers wound their way serenely to the newly created market center at Abilene. Not a hostile Indian was sighted on the trip, and no untoward event occurred to mar its success. Even the weather was most favorable. Usually the country is deluged with heavy spring and summer rains and there are swollen streams to swim, but there was no more precipitation than was needed to keep the grass luxuriantly fresh and tender and to keep a plentiful supply of water at all times. It can be said that this was the last time the word of Joseph McCoy was ever questioned by a Texas cattleman. In the years to come, he was a prime factor in the trade, and he commanded the respect and confidence of every cowman who went up the trail.

With a promoter's zeal for publicity, McCoy could not let this opportunity slip by. As quickly as he and Thompson reached an agreement, he took to horse and hastened back to Abilene. He informed the world by telegraph of the coming event and set about to present his show. Upon the day the herd was due to arrive, he induced the railroad company to run a special train loaded with packinghouse representatives and speculators from the stockyards and cattle feeders from the farm belt. Attached to the rear of the train were private cars of rail officials. Included in the crowd was a brass band of a dozen pieces capable of producing music of the fastest tempo to give the occasion proper zest. McCoy erected a bandstand in the center of the town and it was ready. Abilene had staged a mushroom growth since the railroad began operations. Many sod houses sheltered newly arrived families, and there were at least a dozen business places, including ever present saloons. A large and rambling building had been erected to serve as a hotel, and the proprietor waited hopefully for the trade that was to come.

McCoy had planned for the herd to pass through the town in a grand parade before proceeding to the loading pens. Thompson knew his Longhorns and what they might do, and he demurred at this part of the arrangement. On the other hand, he realized that he was under a great obligation to McCoy, and he did not have the heart to refuse point-blank. He admitted it was McCoy's show and that the promoter was justly entitled to his moment of glory. Once more that hard-pressed man from down in the cattle ranges of Texas fell under McCoy's persuasive influence when he agreed to drive the herd through town.

Whipping his herd together a mile away, Thompson and his men stretched them into a trailing line. Neither the town of Abilene nor any other town in the world had ever witnessed a more impressive sight. Wild cattle, with rocking chairs of horns held aloft upon their upraised heads, marched toward the little hamlet upon the open prairie. On they came, with ears aquiver and nostrils distended, sniffing at the unfamiliar odors, such as stables and domestic pets, and a conglomeration of human beings. With their large eyes wide with awe and flashing with terror at the strange sight of buildings and wagons and teams and people, two thousand long-horned steers marched into the single street of Abilene.

The townspeople had been warned of the danger of a stampede. In spite of this, the entire population crowded doorways and lined the sidewalks. It was a sight worth seeing. Two thousand wild steers walked into the village. They were herded by twenty bearded and picturesque men from the distant cattle ranges, who wore boots and spurs, and wide-brimmed hats, and leather chaps, and Colt frontier six-shooters swinging in their belts. On through the street the uneasy cattle came, crowding and shuffling against each other, seeking to remove themselves from the unfamiliar and disturbing sights.

Five hundred head passed the open square and the bandstand without a break, and then, the climax came. At a signal from McCoy, the band opened up with its liveliest circus tune, with the slide trombone and snare drum competing for the lead. This was too much for those untamed Longhorns, who had never heard a louder strain of music than a cowboy's whistle. The leaders broke and whirled back and soon the roll caused from pounding hooves drowned out the music. Back they surged, colliding with those that were following. In another moment a sea of surging cattle covered by a forest of horns was aloose and stampeding in the town of Abilene.

Once their fear reached the panic stage, they swept back to freedom, heedless of what might be in their path. The bandstand was the first to crumble as a wave of rushing animals brushed away one corner. The bandsmen had seen the storm and escaped with their lives, but many of them sacrificed their instruments. Teams and wagons were caught in the rush, and vehicles were mashed to the ground, while the horses were swept along with the flood. The corner of a sod store was torn from its roof, leaving a gaping hole where clouds of dry dust blotted the surroundings. Back to the prairie they went, with those hard-riding cowboys in pursuit. In spite of all the excitement and disturbance, there was, fortunately, only one casualty, and it was not serious. One man, who was fleeing across an open lot to the safety of his house, had an arm and some ribs broken when he was struck by a wagon pulled by a runaway team.

The untimely and spectacular end of the celebration cost Thompson and his men another day of hard work. In the general mix-up, the herd had become so scattered and frightened that some of the cattle ran for ten miles before they could be stopped. By the time they were rounded up and returned to the shipping pens it was too late to get them corralled and loaded that day, and the Thompson cowboys had to stand another night guard before they were released from duty.

A few cattle were injured to the extent that they could not be shipped, but they were not a total loss. The only people who were not satisfied with the outcome of the event were the storekeeper, whose building was crushed, and the farmers who had their wagons smashed to the ground during the stampede. McCoy stood good for the loss and damage to the musicians' instruments, and in time he appeased all losers.

True to his word, McCoy produced a number of buyers who were anxious to invest and speculate in Texas cattle. In fact, many of them were disappointed because the Thompson herd had been sold before it ever reached Abilene. Three stockmen formed a partnership and met the herd down the trail and contracted for the cattle to be delivered on board the railroad cars. Abilene was established as a market center, and the feasibility of driving through the Indian Territory was proven. The buyers who failed to purchase cattle laid plans for another day. All parties were highly pleased with the results, and the happiest man among them was Joe McCoy.

CHAPTER FIVE

COWTOWNS
COMB THEIR HAIR

THE Thompson herd was not the only one shipped from Abilene the year of its opening. McCoy again took to horse for the purpose of diverting cattle to his own shipping point. His efforts were not without success. He intercepted a number of herds bound for the Baxter Springs area and managed to swing some of them his way. Before the season closed, thirty-five thousand head had walked up through the loading chutes into the cars at Abilene. With what he had already accomplished, and with prospects for the future, McCoy considered a year's work well done.

It was gratifying news that Thompson and other drovers brought back to Texas that fall. Like Indian smoke signals relayed from hill to hill, the word spread from the Red River to the Rio Grande. It was too late in the season to take advantage of the newly opened route that year, but extensive plans were laid out for the next. Those who wavered at the risk of driving through Indians lands overcame their doubts and cast their lot with the new movement. Strange to say, the dreaded menace of the Indians proved to be without foundation. The Army had been proceeding in its slow, but effective way, and the Indians had learned that punishment was sure and certain when they indulged themselves in large-scale depredations. They had also learned to fear those hard-riding and straight-shooting men of the cattle country, and there was never a pitched battle between cowmen and Indians on the Kansas Trail.

The year 1868 saw the heaviest movement of cattle that had ever been driven over a single route up to that time. More than a quarter of a million animals crossed Red River and followed the Chisholm Trail to the Kansas border and thence to Abilene. Many cattlemen, who feared the market would not stand up under such a heavy onslaught, jumped the gun by making an early start in an attempt to get there first. Great herds from the Gulf Coast region and from lower reaches of the Brazos and the Colorado were on the trail and moving northward before the break of winter. From early summer until flying snow in the fall, loading crews at the Abilene shipping pens worked day and night, passing on an endless stream of cattle which taxed their own and the railroad's facilities to keep up with the rush.

McCoy had gone to considerable length to advertise the town of Abilene, but his publicity was directed solely to prospective cattle buyers. While he was working from his own angle, the railroad was working from another. The entire region held promise of becoming an excellent farming country, and not wishing to rely altogether upon the cattle trade for revenues, the railroad directed its advertising campaign toward prospective homeseekers. They did not, by any means, attempt to keep secret the great prosperity of the cattle business, and this was the element that caught the popular fancy.

And to Abilene and its environs came every class of beings known to the human race. If the town's growth up to 1867 had been remarkable, it was now phenomenal. Enterprising businessmen, shrewd and close-fisted Yankee traders, saloon keepers, gamblers, thieves and robbers, along with the painted fancy women who were there for purposes of their own — all of these added their numbers to the town's population. Civic-minded townsmen laid out streets and named them. Money flowed as freely as water in the Smoky Hill, and it looked like everybody in the whole universe was either there, or on his way, for the purpose of dipping his hands into the pots of gold. Into the midst of this aggregation rode the picturesque horsemen from the Southwest, who had cut their teeth upon fighting weapons and who were almost as wild as the cattle they drove over the trail. These consisted of every type of their own kind. Some were good, and some were bad, but none were timid. No fainthearted man would have braved the dangers and withstood the rigors of that long trail. They rolled them high, wide and handsome, with all bars down and the sky the limit.

Into this Devil's cesspool ventured another class of people, as different from all the others as day is from night. These were strait-laced and religious folk, who came to Abilene for the purpose of making permanent homes in the town and surrounding country. They were courageous, too, or they would never have risked themselves in such an environment. From the beginning, they were outspoken in their dislike for the evils of the town and for those who thrived upon it. They centered their principal objections, which were not altogether free from envy, upon the proud and reckless horsemen who asked odds or favors of no one. These people engaged in trade and farming, and in spite of their sanctimony, they were willing to pick up any of the sinful money that came their way. As their numbers increased, they exerted more influence upon the affairs of the town and country and, in time, they were to triumph in their crusade and assume absolute control of community affairs.

For a short while, Abilene was free and unrestrained. During the shipping season, saloons and gambling halls ran wide open, day and night. Unrestricted drinking and gambling were indulged in freely by most citizens, and at times the streets blazed with pistol fire from guns in the hands of cowboys as they staged wild celebrations. Strange to say, no killing occurred until the reform element took steps to enforce law and order. In time the leading citizens of the town organized a local government by election of a mayor and council. Ordinances were adopted and the next logical step was the appointment of a city marshal.

The selection of a marshal was easier said than done. Anyone with gumption enough to fill the office knew that when he attempted to enforce the newly created ordinances, he was literally taking his life in his own hands. Eventually, they located a man who said he could handle the situation, but he did not suit exactly. He told them his name was Smith, but that he always went by the name of Bear River Tom. He had sojourned in the town a few days before making his application and, during that time, he had patronized the bars and gambling tables the same as anyone else. The town rulers could not stomach such behavior and the application was rejected.

They succeeded in locating another applicant who seemed to qualify in every way. He was a total abstainer and shunned all places of evil. Subsequent developments proved that he was lacking in courage, which was the principal element for a law-enforcement officer. His name is unknown, but it makes little difference. His tenure of office was short, and his deeds hardly worth recording. One of his first acts was to tack up posters at different places stating that it was illegal for anyone but himself to carry firearms within the city limits. Bullets from the guns he intended to silence soon obliterated the printing, and not a single weapon was turned over to responsible persons by the owner.

In the meantime, the erection of a jail was started. It was placed on Texas Street, and the boys from the South took this matter as an insult. Before the building was half completed, a crowd of hilarious men leveled it to the ground under cover of darkness. This caused great indignation among the self-styled "better class" of people in the town, who threatened dire recriminations. Another structure was hastily built on the same spot, under an armed guard day and night. Now the new jail was ready to receive its first prisoner.

One of the principal reasons for the enmity that existed between the cowmen and the citizens of Abilene was the opposite stand they had taken during the late war. This feeling seemed more in evidence among the Abilenians than the cowmen. The Texans were not, according to the Kansans, as submissive as a vanquished foe should be, and the townspeople resented their independence. To furnish added fuel to the smoldering fire, those cowboys who rode their horses up and down the streets looked down upon any person who tilled the soil or engaged in menial labor for his living. There has always been a certain amount of arrogance befitting a person on horseback. No matter what station in life a foot man may hold, his pride and self-esteem are enhanced immediately when he seats himself astride a horse. This fact has been true down through the length of history, and it is true to this day. The Texans had been riding horses for many years, and they had a historical background to support them.

But the reformers were determined to have law and order, and in the city marshal they had their necessary tool to secure it. It is a strange fact that the first inmate of the Abilene jail was a member of a race that the Kansans had fought a war to free. A Negro cook employed by one of the cow outfits took on a generous load of talking water and decided to show his skill with a firearm just as he had seen the cowboys do. He took some fancy potshots at different objects on the street, and this gave the new marshal the chance he had been looking for. From the manner in which other things had come about, one is led to believe that this move was made to test out sentiment and get a reaction. The town officials had been a little dubious about attempting to arrest a cowboy. They feared it might result in a fatal gunfight, and that was the thing they wished, by all means, to avoid. They seemed to think nobody would make a fuss about the arrest of a colored man.

If this was the way they reasoned things out, they made a bad guess. They still did not understand the nature of their Texans. If the most prominent cattle baron who ever drove a herd or bossed a roundup had been thrown into jail, the act would not have caused more indignation. "They take their spite out on a helpless nigger. They'll find out we'll fight for our niggers the same as for ourselves," were some of the indignant remarks. Word of the brazen insult was carried from one cow outfit to another camped around town and, shortly after dark, fifty armed and mounted men were converging upon Abilene.

They surrounded the jail and rode circles around it, Indian-fashion. No band of Indians ever made more noise than those rescuing cowboys as they punctuated their wild yells with pistol shots. The townspeople were convinced that the day of destruction was at hand, and the unnamed marshal was not to be found. It was discovered later that he was hiding in the darkest corner of a saloon while the fracas was going on. Some of the deliverers dismounted and, using a detached wagon tongue as a battering ram, they soon had the jail door sagging on its hinges. The inmate of the jail first cowered in one corner, but when he heard the familiar voices and glimpsed the horsemen, he met them with a wide grin upon his face. His first words were, "Praise God — mah friends ah heah."

Regardless of how much they were all afraid the night before, things looked different next morning. The city rulers felt that the marshal should have stopped the jail delivery, and for his failure to do so, he was run off the job. Fearing they were in for a reign of terror at the hands of wild cowboys, the mayor advertised frantically for another peace officer. Tempted by the offer of high wages, several prospects looked the job over, but turned it down. Bear River Tom had migrated to other parts, but the mayor succeeded in locating him and sent him an urgent message to come. The offer was accepted, and when the new marshal took over his duties, he pulled a trick that no one expected to see.

Bear River was tall and muscular and he moved about with the litheness and precision of a panther. He went about his duties as unassumingly as though they were the most commonplace assignment. The cowboys had been running wild for a long time, and it was inevitable that the two forces would come together. When they did, the marshal found himself up against one of the toughest men who ever looked through a gunsight. He profanely dared Bear River to disarm him, and his manner indicated he was itching to draw the gun that was hanging in his belt. Bear River did not flinch from the threat. He only moved a step closer to it. Then, with the suddenness of a rattlesnake strike, his fist shot out and caught the rebellious cowboy squarely on the jaw. When the latter came to, Bear River had extracted his gun from its holster and was standing over him with a grin on his face. All the cowboy did was to rub his jaw and walk away. He never sought revenge, and he was never known to carry a gun upon the streets as long as Bear River held the post of marshal.

With the exception of one other occurrence, this put a quietus on disturbances. The Texans knew nothing about that kind of fighting, and they dreaded Bear River's fists more than they did his gun. There was some consolation in the thought of dying bravely in a gunfight, but it certainly was a stigma to be knocked out by a fist. The Texans got some satisfaction, however, when a stranger drifted into town and listened incredulously to the stories about the prowess of the marshal. He was not a Western man and certainly not a cowboy, but he rated himself as being a little tougher than anyone else. He said he knew all about fistfighting and that no hack of a town marshal could back him down. He said that his knuckles were just itching for a whack at that overrated pugilist. It was not long before he got his chance, and it is said that Bear River put him to sleep for a longer period than he had the cowboy. The Texans got considerable satisfaction out of that conflict. Up to that time, they had been ashamed to know that anyone had bluffed them out with his fists. Now, here was a man who claimed to be an expert and Bear River had laid him low. It was not so shameful now to recognize his authority, and they willingly checked in their guns to responsible parties when they arrived in town.

But fate was ready to deliver Bear River Tom an unkind blow. He did not lose his life at the hands of the cowboy or any of the lawless element of the town; his death came about by a member of the group who had been instrumental in hiring him as a marshal. Two farmers had a misunderstanding and one killed the other. When Bear River went forth to make the arrest, he was waylaid and shot from ambush. He was given less consideration and less chance for his life than he would have received from one of the cowboys had they met in battle.

Once more Abilene sank back into the old sinful rut, and the town became wilder than ever. It was like releasing floodwaters by a broken dam. The council and mayor decided to do things up in fine style and hire an expert gunman. They had heard of a courageous man and dangerous gunfighter who went by the name of Wild Bill Hickok. They made their offer sufficiently tempting to induce the famous trigger man to accept the duties of their city marshal.

Wild Bill restored order to the town in a short time, even though he had to kill a few men to do so. At that he was not feared by the Texans in the way they had dreaded Bear River Tom. Wild Bill fought with guns the same as they, too, and even though the loser did usually pay with his life, it was not too shameful to lie down in the face of a gun. Wild Bill relented in the rule that no one but himself was permitted to carry firearms. He had no fear of any armed man, and he could see no sense in imposing the rule. He drank and gambled as freely as anyone else, but he carried out his duties.

His career as city marshal of Abilene was short, and it ended with a double killing. He and a gambler came to gun points, and as usual, Wild Bill was the winner. During the mix-up and excitement, he unwittingly killed his deputy and best friend, who had been attracted by the gunfire and who came running to the scene. After this fatal episode, Wild Bill was relieved of his post. Events were shaping up to where it made little difference now, however. The cattle trade was shifting to other points and the Abilene reformers had a full opportunity to run their town as they saw fit.

While different elements were struggling for power to rule the town, an endless stream of homesteaders was coming to the country. They were settling upon land in all directions and some started farms which lay squarely across the cattle trail. These new arrivals prospered from the sale of garden and dairy products, which were in great demand by the cattlemen. Regardless of the money the cattlemen spent with them, it did not wipe out that age-old enmity existing between herdsmen and tillers of the soil.

From 1868 to 1870, cattle poured over the trail into Abilene. There was a mounting hostility among the farmers against what they deemed to be intrusion. Eventually matters came to a point where the farmers decided to take action to stop it. They held many meetings and worked up public sentiment against the cattle trade. They passed resolutions and published them widely, demanding that the trail men keep their herds a certain distance from any occupied or cultivated farm. Such action would shut the gate upon the shipping point. For a short time the peace-maker McCoy was able to mollify them by pointing out the pros-perity brought by the cattlemen, but they soon turned a deaf ear to his pleadings. In 1871 the farmers brought pressure to bear upon the businessmen of Abilene and persuaded a majority to join them in the move. This resulted in scathing denunciation of the cattle trade, and circulars were scattered over the cattle country of Texas, advising the cattlemen they were no longer wanted at Abilene, and suggesting that they take their business elsewhere. This was the death song of the Abilene cattle market.

The decisive and hostile action did not catch the Texas cat-tlemen unawares by any means. They had seen the handwriting upon the wall for some time, and they were making ready to switch their drives elsewhere. Indeed, many of them had already done so, before the resolutions and warning were circulated. After receiving the official, and final, notice, the others quit cold in 1872. Not one carleed of Texas cattle was shipped from Abilene that year.

The cattle trade was not through by any means. The Kansas Pacific Railroad had extended its line farther west, and the little village of Ellsworth was selected as the new shipping point. For the first time, the railroad showed some interest in the cattle trade, and the company erected its own shipping pens. They were constructed on a lavish scale and even outranked those built by McCoy at Abilene. No doubt there was truth in the claim that they were the finest in the world. They boasted of seven loading chutes, and a yard that would easily hold five thousand cattle. The railroad company's contract with McCoy applied to Abilene only, and he was shut out from the Ellsworth deal entirely. He lived to have the satisfaction of pulling the cattle trade away from the Kansas Pacific to another road, where he once more built his own shipping pens and mingled and counselled with the cattlemen again.

Too late, the businessmen of Abilene saw the blunder they had made in driving the cattle business away from their doors. They discovered that those strait-laced farmers, who were so long on piety, were very short on ready cash. The prosperity of the stores had come directly from the cattlemen, or indirectly from them through the farmers. Now that was gone. The farmers no longer had a market for their produce and they turned out to be very poor customers indeed. In desperation, the businessmen offered inducements to their former customers for a return of the good old days, but their cause was a lost one.

It could be expected that the gamblers, saloon keepers, and inmates of the houses of ill fame would follow the cattle trade, but it was a clear example of human vicissitude when those resolving businessmen of Abilene pulled up stakes and moved over to the new town. Most of the frame houses of the former shipping point were transported across the prairie to Ellsworth. Those that were immovable were deserted and their owners set up shop in newly erected buildings. Soon the town of Abilene lapsed back into the sleepy little village of five years before, when Joseph McCoy waved his wand over it and made it the cattle capital of the world.

The high life of Ellsworth was short, but things were painted red while they lasted. For two years the cattle came and the history of the town was much more lurid and bloody than that of Abilene. The killings were chiefly between gamblers and law-enforcement officers, some of whom ranked in morals little above the lowest elements. The one exception was the tragic death of the sheriff, who held the respect of everyone, including the toughest men who ever straddled a horse or turned a card at a gambling table. The sheriff met his death at the hands of a friend and admirer through the accidental discharge of a shotgun, which was intended to be used on another clique of rival gamblers. As accustomed as those desperate men were to violence, and as cheaply as they held human life, the killing of the sheriff cast a pall upon the whole community. It also heralded a clean-up drive against all undesirable characters. Before the effect of the reform was really felt, the cattle trade was slipping away to other parts.

Like nearly any other business, the cattle trade was not bound by any hard-and-fast rules. Drovers were constantly seeking the shortest and most convenient routes to market, and the Santa Fe Railroad was making that provision. Their tracks had been laid west to Newton, which was nearly a hundred miles closer to the great Texas ranges than either Abilene or Ellsworth. The line also projected into a country where the annoying nesters — as homesteaders had come to be called — had not gained a foothold, and to Newton went the cattle trade.

Here we see the hand of Joseph McCoy at work again. After being shut out by the Kansas Pacific Railroad, he negotiated a deal with the Santa Fe for livestock shipments, something on the order of his first arrangement at Abilene. The Texans were glad to re-establish their old relationship, because McCoy performed a valuable service in his capacity of livestock agent by ordering cars for the shippers and making other arrangements with the railroads.

For a time Newton served as the cattle capital of the world. Its reign was short, but the town's history was the bloodiest of all up to that time. More killings occurred in Newton during the year of its cattle trade than in both Abilene and Ellsworth put together. The slayings were not confined to gamblers and peace officers by any means. Many cowboys' lives were sacrificed to the quick-triggered elements of the town. To cap it off, several of the local citizens reached disagreements and settled their differences at gun point. It seems that, more and more, attempts at regulation and law enforcement resulted in more shooting scrapes. The larger the police force, the larger the boot-hill graveyard.

The Santa Fe rails soon reached the village of Wichita, which completed the circle. It was from here that Jesse Chisholm, the Indian trader, laid out his memorable trail down through the Indian country. It was his trail which the first herds followed to the Kansas border and then branched off to Abilene and Ellsworth. Now, they followed it from one end to the other. Here we find Joe McCoy again, who had seen the trend of affairs and was ready with adequate stockyards when the cattle arrived.

For two years Wichita held the spotlight of the cattle trade with a comparable bloody history. During this time the Santa Fe had been extending its line westward from Newton, and now the business moved on to the grandpappy of them all, Dodge City. Incidentally, this is the last we hear of Joseph McCoy. As the Kansas Pacific had done at Ellsworth, the Santa Fe shut him out from the new shipping point at Dodge City. For eight years he had followed the trade from one cowtown to another, and he left his influence upon the business.

A pitiful story could be told about Joseph McCoy. His rise to fame and fortune was as meteoric as a soaring rocket and his downfall came with as much suddenness. His failure in business could never be attributed to the Texas cattlemen, however. From the time the trail driver Thompson committed himself and his fortune into McCoy's hands when they met on that trackless prairie down in the Indian Territory in 1867, his integrity was never questioned. Windy and boastful as he was, he always made his promises good. His word to the cattlemen proved to be as solid as a foundation, and how those cowmen respected another who made his word good at any cost! McCoy attributed his downfall to the railroad companies' failure to keep their own obligations. He had become so accustomed to relying upon word promises that he failed to have his dealings with the railroads bound up by written contract. If the Texas cattlemen had been the kind to give way to sentiment, they would have erected a monument to his memory.

Now to Dodge City came the cattle trade. The Chisholm Trail, which had been the roadway for more than a million cattle for the last eight years, was abandoned. There was a brief lapse when the Rock Island built into southern Kansas to Caldwell, but the number of cattle that traveled the trail was almost negligible after Dodge City was opened up in 1875. Some of the deep ruts cut by sharp hooves are still visible on the prairie, but that is all. A monument on the Chisholm Trail, now and then, has been erected by the patriotic people of Oklahoma, to commemorate its founder, but the cattle trail has nothing left but a vanishing memory.

For at least twenty grand and glorious years Dodge City was the center of all cattle attractions. A new trail running due north from Red River crossing was laid out to the wild cowtown. Over this route, which became known as the Texas Trail, came millions of other cattle to eclipse those passing over the Chisholm route. This trail was the answer to a trail driver's prayer. It ran straight across the wide open prairie unmarred by a farmer's plow. It was the kind of a trail that cowmen hoped would last forever.

At Dodge City, lawlessness reached its climax. It was said there was no law west of Newton, and no God west of Dodge, which came near to being the truth. Men with reputations as killers, with many notches upon their gun handles, visited the place and frankly admitted it to be the toughest spot they had ever seen. Another element heretofore unknown injected itself into the conglomeration of many classes of men at Dodge City. The death knell of the great buffalo herds that roamed the plains had already been sounded when the buffalo hunters and skinners took to the field. Dodge City became the headquarters and shipping point for all hides of the entire Southern area. The peace and dignity of the community was not improved a particle when those roughly dressed, bearded, and uncouth plainsmen, with their faces blackened from gunpowder smoke, stalked the streets. The hard-faced and cold-blooded men who followed the trade of peace officers had their hands full in their efforts to preserve law and order. Many a life was snuffed out in the flash of gunfire, and the boot-hill cemetery of Dodge City was the largest of them all.

The life of Dodge City as a cattle center was the longest, the liveliest, the wickedest and the bloodiest of all other cow-towns that had ever blossomed. It is true that since the Abilene market had opened up, there had been a gradual change and slacking off in certain areas. What might be termed the old cattle-breeding grounds of southern Texas were becoming shut off from a trail outlet by the same forces that had closed the gate on Abilene. Farmers and small ranchers had pushed westward across the eastern and central part of the state in such numbers that it became extremely difficult and expensive to thread a large herd back and forth through them. Some railroads had laid their tracks into that part of the country, which did away with the necessity of making the long trail drive to market the stock. Thus, by the time Dodge established herself as the cattle capital, the region of South Texas that had contributed so heavily to the first cowtowns was sliding back down the trail, never to return.

The fact that South and East Texas eliminated themselves from trail driving did not interfere with the greatness of Dodge City. Those wide expanses along the Canadian, the Cimarron, both forks of the Red, and the upper reaches of the Brazos and Colorado were producing cattle by the thousands and hundreds of thousands. From all this territory the trails were open to Dodge City, and they were extensively used. Indeed, the shipping point drew trade from deep in southern New Mexico. It was not uncommon to see John Chisum's cowboys, bearing dust upon their hat brims gathered from the alkali flats of the Pecos, riding through the streets.

But the cattle which came to Dodge City for shipment were not the only ones to approach the town. Contrary to the opinions of many who thought trail driving was on its last legs, the profession was just getting started. The great ranges of the Northwest were being stocked and re-stocked, and for twenty years cattle flowed past Dodge City in a never ending stream during the summer season. The outfits from all over North and West Texas and eastern New Mexico paused in the surrounding country long enough to renew supplies of food and other necessities, while those cowboys who wished to do so broke the monotony of long and arduous days in the saddle with a well-earned celebration. It is safe to say that more cattle have been herded within sight of the buildings in Dodge City than in any other town in the world.

CHAPTER SIX
FROM THE PECOS
TO THE PLATTE

THIS treatise was never intended to be a means of glorifying any certain individual. The cattle industry was so large in its scope that to make a list of those deserving credit and honorable mention would be next to impossible. Many an unknown man came upon the scene and fulfilled his mission, only to fade back into obscurity. Many a man sacrificed his life to the undertaking without his deeds or name being recorded in the annals of history. As an example there is the drover Thompson, who delivered the first herd to Abilene. Outside of the fact that he was one of the hard-pressed cowmen with more cattle than money, little is known about him. His name does not appear in the record of later events. Had it not been for scant writings left by Joseph McCoy, it is doubtful if Thompson's name would be known at this time.

On the other hand, it is impossible to compile an account of such a vast undertaking where individualism and self-reliance formed the very keystone of the foundation, without certain men creeping into the limelight in spite of the recorder's desire to keep them anonymous. As an example, there is the promoter Joseph McCoy. This man was not a cowman by any means, but he certainly wielded a strong influence upon the industry in its early stages. The deplorable part of McCoy's career was his financial failure when he had achieved his goal; still, no one can truthfully say that his life work was a failure. From what is known of his character, it would appear that his efforts were directed toward a great accomplishment rather than toward financial gain. If such is the case, they were crowned with success. It is safe to say that as he looked back over the past and realized fulfillment of his dreams by seeing the great herds of cattle moving across the wide prairies toward his shipping point, he received his reward in the comforting knowledge of work well done, even though he viewed the scene from the shoes of a financial failure.

Mention has been made of John Chisum, of whom there will be more. Later in this work will appear the name of John Blocker, who is credited with being the foremost trail driver who ever piloted a herd. Now comes the time to introduce the most outstanding of all cowmen — Charles Goodnight. There is McCoy the promoter, John Chisum the great rancher and John Blocker the wise trail man; but Charles Goodnight was a combination of them all, and he excelled in all phases of the calling. The deeds of this great man would fill a huge volume and still the account would not do him justice. There will be no dispute of a statement by those who know that his individual efforts and initiative did more to develop the cattle business than did the efforts of any other since the time when the first straggling bunches were branded up to the present day. Neither is there any doubt but that more cattle passed through his hands than through those of any other living man. It is safe to say that during his lifetime he handled more than a quarter of a million head.

In later years he was accused of being ruthless and domineering, with a self-serving ambition for power and riches. Old acquaintances charged that, with his ascension to financial success, he laid aside former precepts and forgot old friendships to which he had been so loyal in the past. Even if true, those faults would never erase the generous deeds of other times when he was ready and willing to sacrifice life and fortune for country or friend.

In early life, Goodnight was both patriotic and unselfish. After reaching a comfortable station of financial success, he was never too much occupied with his own affairs to take time out and serve as a scout for an expedition by either the Texas Rangers or the United States Army against the Indians. Indeed, he was an active member of the Rangers during those troublesome years when fighting men were badly needed. He was reputed to have been the best scout who ever followed an Indian trail, and his sagacity saved more than one punitive expedition from failure, and more than one party from death by starvation. In the semi-arid and uncharted regions of the Staked Plains and in the wide areas between the Cap Rock and the Pecos, he either knew where the watering places were located, or how they could be found. His wisdom was based on a close observation and study of nature, which gave him the ability to read signs in the sky and interpret the moods and actions of wild animals and of fowls of the air. The early years of his life were divided between a struggle to earn a living and to protect his modest holdings and those of his neighbors against Indian depredations. Neither was he without sentiment. A story is told of a certain cow that escaped from a herd during one of Goodnight's drives to New Mexico and made her way alone for three hundred miles back to the ranch. When he discovered her on his return, he ordained that she should be allowed to live out the remainder of her life in the land that she loved so well.

Before the outbreak of the War Between the States, Charles Goodnight was engaged in ranching in a modest way. He secured a partner and they tended a small bunch of cattle, while Goodnight occasionally augmented the firm's income by freighting goods with ox teams deep into the inland. He was one who dared the Indians by establishing himself on the frontier past the safety zone of forts in order that his business would not be handicapped by lack of room for expansion. By the time hostilities broke out, he had grown a sizable herd of cattle, but the war seriously disrupted his affairs and retarded his financial development.

While Goodnight never donned the uniform of the Confederacy, he served the state and his neighbors during the war far better than had he sacrificed his life upon an eastern battlefield. He was on the verge of enlisting when he suffered a serious injury. By the time he recovered, he had come to the conclusion that he had best stay out of the army. It cannot be said that any element of cowardice or selfishness influenced his decision. He immediately joined up with the Rangers, who were sorely pressed to hold the tides of Indian warriors away from the settlements. He abandoned his ranch and left his cattle to what care his neighbors might be able to give them. Since all able-bodied men were eventually drawn away from home to one battleground or the other, women and children were the only ones left to take care of things. Consequently, Goodnight's cattle scattered here and there and went unbranded and untended.

At the end of the war, Goodnight returned to find his buildings destroyed and his cattle scattered, with many of them wearing brands of others. After gathering up remnants of his brand and re-locating them upon the range, he turned his hand to any kind of work that would make him an honest dollar. He took advantage of low prices and all the money he managed to accumulate and all the proceeds from credit he was able to establish were invested in cattle. Within a short time he had built up another sizable herd. While most cattlemen were groping in the darkness and uncertainties of the Ozark and Baxter Springs trails, he cast his gaze in another direction. He saw a grand opportunity unfolding and, after due consideration, took advantage of it.

The United States Government was undertaking to keep all Indians upon their reservations. Since the measure would cut those in the western half of New Mexico off from the buffalo, which was their main food source, the Government entered into a treaty with the Navajo and Ute tribes to supply them with beef for immediate consumption and a stock for future needs. It was hoped that they would eventually become self-supporting by the production of their own beef for food. This measure proved only partly successful. While the Indians were willing to take anything of value that was given to them, it was difficult to make them see the need of saving a few breeding cows as a foundation herd for future use. It was to be many years before they became self-supporting by producing their own livestock.

In carrying out the above policy, the Government offered contracts for delivery of large numbers of cattle to the Indian agency in New Mexico. There were very few, if any, cattle at all in that territory, and the supply had to be drawn from Texas. There were no cattle in Texas west of the Colorado, which was some five hundred miles from the point of delivery. The prices offered by the contracts were extremely good and promised satisfactory returns to anyone who fulfilled them. On the other hand, serious obstacles lay in the way. In order to reach the designated place in New Mexico from the cattle-producing areas of Texas, it was necessary to drive a hundred miles across a high plain between the Concho and Pecos rivers, an area which in normal times was without water. This question provoked many discussions among experienced cattlemen as to whether it was possible to make such a drive with a large herd.

But the lack of water over a long stretch of the route was not the only, and far from the most serious danger confronting an aspiring trail man. He would be exposing himself and his property to the boldest and most rapacious Indian tribes that inhabited the American plains. The United States Army had been partly successful in separating these warring tribes by pushing the Comanches northeast, and the Apaches westward, but they were not subdued by any means. The Comanches still made daring raids down through the cattle country of the Brazos and the Colorado, leaving a trail of destruction in their wake, while the Apaches roamed the trans-Pecos area and lower regions of the Staked Plains at will. Between Fort Concho in Texas and Fort Sumner in New Mexico, a distance of nearly four hundred miles, a trail man would be strictly on his own.

There is some disagreement among authorities as to whether Charles Goodnight or John Chisum was the first to travel the Pecos Trail. The preponderance of evidence seems to give the distinction to Goodnight. Before the end of the war, Chisum had moved his herds from Northeast Texas out into the Indian country at the mouth of the Concho, which act evidenced a total disregard for danger. He settled himself beyond what was considered the safety zone, away from the jurisdiction of carpetbag courts and politicians during Reconstruction days, since he regarded them as a greater menace than the Indians. Although Chisum moved into New Mexico in a short time, the best evidence is that he was still located at the mouth of the Concho, debating the feasibility of taking the risk, when Goodnight passed by with his first herd.

Before reaching a decision and entering into a contract to supply beef at the Indian agency, Goodnight weighed all contingencies. The prospects of huge profits were sufficient to tempt a heedless man into direct commitment, but no one realized the risks involved in such a venture better than he did. He had fought Indians the major part of his life and he knew what they would do if given an opportunity. His conclusion was that he could work secretly and get started before the Indians learned of his intentions and had time to organize a force of warriors strong enough to constitute a threat. Since he was a fighting man himself and had selected only brave and trustworthy men to accompany the expedition, he had no fear but that they would be able to beat off any roving bands that might chance upon them by accident. This line of reasoning proved correct. The first trip, with three thousand cattle in the herd, was entirely successful. He delivered them to the Indian agency and reaped his reward in a handsome profit.

With a full force of men and saddle horses, and with wagons heavily loaded with provisions for the six hundred-mile trip, he started upon the long and perilous journey. Out through the rugged hills flanking the Brazos and on to the rolling prairies of the Colorado watershed he moved. Up the Concho the herd drifted leisurely past the John Chisum camp at the mouth of that stream, where the Chisum cowboys, with six-shooters on their belts and Winchesters in their saddle scabbards, rode wide circles over the range, guarding the Long Rail and Jingle Bob cattle from the depredations of roving Comanches.

Goodnight spent some time counseling with Chisum and laying plans for making the drive across the dry divide between the Concho and the Pecos. Up to that time, Chisum's experience as a trail man greatly eclipsed that of Goodnight. He had gained much knowledge about trailing cattle during the war when he drove many herds through to the Confederate Army along the Mississippi. Chisum frankly admitted during their discussions that the Pecos country was his own goal, but that he had not seen his way clear to take the chance of losing a herd from starvation upon the waterless divide, nor to the Apaches when he reached their land.

With the advice offered by Chisum still alive in his memory, Goodnight moved his herd on to the headwaters of the Concho. Here, he called a halt and rested upon abundant grass and water for two days. At high noon of the second day, with the cattle and saddle horses fully watered and all available barrels in the wagons filled to capacity, he pointed the herd westward toward the top of the high divide hazy with distance.

The first night after leaving the Concho was the last time that men, or horses or cattle had any rest until the Pecos was reached, a hundred miles away. The second night the high divide was topped and they turned downhill into a winding draw that sank deeper into the prairie with each mile covered. For four more days and nights the long herd wound its way along the dry trail toward the Pecos. For four more days and nights it stretched out longer and thinner as the strong animals in the lead gradually pulled away from the weaker ones in the drag. For four more days and nights, Charles Goodnight and his men rode anxiously back and forth along that crawling line, holding the leaders back and urging the rear ones on. At last the Pecos was reached, and with fewer losses than had been expected. After a deserved rest upon water and grass the herd moved up that stream to Fort Sumner, where delivery was made.

Inspired by the success of the undertaking and with high hopes of making other similar ones, Goodnight sped back to Texas as fast as he and his men could ride the six hundred miles and move the outfit of wagons and saddle horses. The proceeds of sale from that herd of cattle was carried in gold coin packed upon a mule. Part of this money was owed to financial backers and part of it belonged to neighbors who had entrusted him with what cattle they had for sale, but the major portion belonged to Charles Goodnight as proceeds from his own cattle and profit from the venture.

Nearly all the cattle that Goodnight owned, and that he wished to sell, had been included in the herd driven to New Mexico. He spent the remainder of the year buying up enough additional animals to make up another herd, and by springtime, he was ready to go again. If his first drive had caught the Indians napping, such was not the case with the second one. Before he was more than fifty miles away from the home ranch, the Comanches swooped down upon the outfit during the night and stampeded the herd far and wide.

There was a bitter, running fight that lasted for hours in pitch darkness, amid the confusion of stampeding cattle, yelling savages, and blazing guns. The break of dawn disclosed the bodies of two cowboys, along with a number of Indians, slain in battle. The entire herd was widely scattered throughout the hills and considerable time was required to round it up again before any idea could be formed as to the number that were missing. After two days of hard riding, it was found that at least half of the animals were gone. In the meantime, while his men were rounding up the scattered cattle, Goodnight had scouted the trail left by the fleeing Indians. It led straight northwest to the breaks along the foot of the Cap Rock, and he ascertained that the force was far too strong for him and his men to engage in battle in an attempt to recover the stolen cattle.

He dismissed the loss with a gesture and delayed the drive long enough to buy additional animals to fill the depleted herd. After reaching the Pecos, they were assailed again and again by raiding bands of Apaches, almost to the limits of the military reservation at Fort Sumner. While the Apache raids were seriously annoying, they were not nearly so devastating and costly as was the one inflicted upon them by the Comanches back in Texas.

Nevertheless, it was a great relief to the owner and a tired crew of men when the final turnover was made after three months of grueling trail work.

While the losses sustained from that disastrous trip crippled Goodnight financially, he was not in the mood to admit failure. He had enough confidence in his men and in himself to believe that they could eventually play a winning hand. There were huge profits to be made, and he shaped his course accordingly. For the purpose of bolstering his credit and to have someone to share part of the responsibility, he deemed it a wise course at this time to secure a partner for future operations.

He interested Oliver Loving, a man somewhat older than he, who was sound financially, thoroughly schooled in the art of handling cattle and wise in Indian warfare. Goodnight termed him to be the best, the bravest, and the most learned cattleman he ever saw. Indeed, it was Loving's extreme bravery that brought about his death when he received a fatal wound in battle with Apache Indians along the Pecos Trail in New Mexico.

The death of Loving was a severe loss for Goodnight, and it seriously affected him in more ways than one. At that time finances of the firm were not in a healthy condition, but Goodnight gritted his teeth and carried on alone. As proof of the kind of a man he was, it is fitting to say that he continued the partnership business by his own efforts for two more years. At the end of that time, he turned over to his dead partner's family forty thousand dollars in gold, which was a sizable fortune for that day. At an appropriate time, he personally supervised the disinterment of Loving's body and transported it by wagon six hundred miles back to the family graveyard.

During the years between 1866 and 1869, Goodnight dominated the New Mexico Indian cattle trade. Other men who were just as brave and just as daring as he saw the huge profits he was making and crowded into the game. Not all were successful by any means, but enough of them got through with their herds to over-supply the market, and the price made a drastic drop. Indeed the stocking of Arizona ranges came about by the surplus of cattle in New Mexico as bold men pushed farther west in search of unlimited cattle range.

While Goodnight gave up the Indian trade in New Mexico, he was not through by any means. In fact, he was just getting started, and he used the trails that he had already opened up as another pathway to greater fortune and glory. Long before the supply exceeded the demand of the New Mexico Indian reservations, he had learned of a desperate need of beef cattle around the mining camps in Colorado. After cutting loose from the New Mexico operations, he pointed a herd northward and moved over the Rocky Mountains through Raton Pass. It was on this trip and at this place that he took his first personal setback and let another man bluff him away from a pre-determined course.

At that time Raton Pass was the only known gateway over the mountains between the Pecos and Arkansas river watersheds. Obstinate old Dick Wootten saw a chance to rake in some easy money and settled himself in the pass to collect a toll of ten cents for each person, animal or vehicle passing through. He had constructed a road of sorts over the crown by his own efforts and at his own expense. He had the foresight to secure legislative authority from the governments of both Colorado and New Mexico to construct the roadway and collect the toll. Besides the legality of his position, he kept a double-barreled shotgun loaded with buckshot at his side as an additional persuasive measure in case some patron turned out to be disagreeable.

Dick Wootten was no tenderfoot or neophite by any means. He had been on the frontier and around mining camps for a number of years and this had brought him up against the toughest men the country had to offer. He had faced dangerous men before, and there was nothing about Goodnight that threw a scare into him. He stated flatly that it would cost Goodnight three hundred dollars cash in hand, and not a cent less, to drive those three thousand cattle through the pass.

Goodnight did not know that Wootten had a legal right to collect the toll, and he could not reconcile himself to letting a man bluff him out of three hundred dollars. On the other hand, there was a gleam in the old squatter's eye that carried a dangerous threat. He had said that he would shoot the first man who put a cow across a designated line without paying him the money, and Goodnight believed he meant every word he said. The matter simmered down in Goodnight's viewpoint to the proposition of either killing the old squatter or being killed himself. He had to move his cattle; therefore, he paid the toll.

While the outcome of the controversy made little difference to Goodnight, the stand proved a costly one for Wootten. Goodnight told him that he would never come that way with another herd; that he would find a way around the toll road. At this bit of defiance Wootten only laughed. He said he knew those hills far better than Goodnight would ever know them, and that there was no other way around. Nevertheless, Goodnight would not be outdone, and his extensive search resulted in the discovery of Trinchera Pass, which is the present roadbed of the Colorado and Southern Railway. This proved to be a better and shorter route to the towns along the foot of the Rockies, and soon all travel was using the Goodnight Trail, which left Dick Wootten sitting high and dry with nothing coming his way.

When Wootten saw his mistake, he offered to pass Goodnight and his cattle free of charge, thinking that others would follow his lead, but Goodnight turned him down. Never again did he use the Raton Pass. In later years those two determined and self-willed men grew to be the best of friends, but their first meeting came near ending in a shooting scrape, which would have been the death of one or the other.

The first cattle drives into Colorado by Goodnight were for the sole purpose of supplying beef to the mining camps. During those first trips he did not fail to see the great possibilities offered by the Colorado ranges for ranching. Indeed, he encountered several men who were anxious to get into the business, and as a result, he formed a connection with a Denver banking group to deliver cattle to them in large numbers. Before long his herds were spreading over the South Platte Valley from the mountains to the Nebraska line, stocking the immense ranches tied together by that pioneer rancher John Iliff and his associates.

The years between 1869 and 1874 were the most spectacular of Goodnight's entire career from the standpoint of a pioneer operation. He drove thousands and thousands of cattle from the breeding grounds of Texas into New Mexico and thence up the Pecos and across the Rockies into Colorado. His contracts were so heavy and demanding that he found it impossible to fulfill them all, and he secured the help of another able cowman. John Chisum had followed him into New Mexico, and Goodnight made arrangements with him to drive cattle from Texas and turn them over at the halfway point along the Pecos. Besides the ones that Chisum drove, Goodnight bought many others from dissatisfied trail men who found themselves stranded in New Mexico on a glutted market.

During this time he engaged in ranching himself on a large scale in the foothills and prairies south and east of Pueblo. As a result of these activities, he amassed a fortune which would be envied by many men even in this day of high finance. He accumulated a financial worth of a quarter of a million dollars, but unfortunately he did not stick to his trade. He allowed himself to be drawn into the banking business on a large scale, besides investing heavily in costly irrigation schemes. The money panics of the Seventies caught him out on a financial limb, and he saw most of his fortune swept away. When the storm was over and the price of his folly was paid, he found himself with only a few thousand dollars and sixteen hundred cattle free of incumbrance. In order to make a recovery, he turned back to the cattle trails he knew so well. Many men would have been satisfied to continue on in a modest way and grow out of the financial disaster with the means at hand, but not so with Charles Goodnight. He had sat in games where stakes were high and he was satisfied with nothing less.

During his scouting days with the Rangers and the army, he had passed through a territory which he deemed to be an ideal cattle country. It was situated south of the Canadian, in the breaks which formed the head of the Red River in Texas. The land had always been the stamping ground of hostile Indians, and no white man had ever risked his life long enough to attempt a location in the country. It was still included in the buffalo range and was the last stronghold of the Comanche Indians who operated in conjunction with the Mexican horse and cattle thieves from around Santa Fe and Las Vegas. Goodnight knew that it would take a strong force of men to guarantee protection of his property against these two marauding bands and that the income from his comparatively small herd of cattle would not bear the expense. For that reason he sought a partner with enough financial standing to operate an outfit large enough to justify assembling a strong force of men.

He re-established himself in the cattle business on a grand scale when he interested a wealthy Englishman as a partner. He returned to Texas and settled in the Palo Duro Canyon in the midst of Indians and buffaloes, where he started one of the most famous ranches in the history of the state. Before he was through, he controlled more than a million acres of land and tens of thousands of cattle. For more than a decade he stood his ground against all adversities with no more law to protect himself and property than what he and his own men could effect themselves. For more than ten years he purchased choice range land from the state and incorporated it into a gigantic holding.

With the coming of organized law to the region and the consolidation of his ranch interests, the spectacular and glamorous career of Charles Goodnight came to an end. From then until the end of his life, he devoted his time to constructive operations along a safe and sane business course. It was during this period that he rendered his most valuable service to the cattle industry. Freed from the threat of Indian raids, he gave his time to experiments in developing a better grade of cattle. Such work is conducted by public institutions at Government expense nowadays, but Goodnight carried on by his own means. He laid the foundation for a brand of cattle that is still in existence and famed for its high quality of breeding.

Charles Goodnight was not the only one who pioneered in establishing the cattle business in the Indian-ridden and dominated wilds of New Mexico. There were others who risked life and fortune in the venture, of whom the most noteworthy was John Chisum. After seeing that it was reasonably safe to drive across the waterless divide to the Pecos, Chisum followed soon after Goodnight had made the first crossing. He drifted his large herd up that stream from where he struck it at the famous and historical Horsehead Crossing in Texas to the Rio Hondo in New Mexico. Here he established his headquarters and elected to engage in ranching and breeding cattle. Outside of his arrangement with Goodnight to drive herds from Texas and turn them over upon arrival, he never indulged in the speculation and trade which was so common among other cowmen.

Chisum divided his force of men and scattered them out in line camps in the best locations for protection of his property. His animals increased in numbers until his Long Rail brand and Jingle Bob mark adorned the hide and ears of seventy-five thousand cattle. They grazed over an area larger than some New England states. He drove herds of steers to various shipping points where a market existed, and the trail from his holdings in New Mexico to Dodge City and other Kansas points was often traveled by himself and his men. He was the first large rancher of record and at that time he laid claim to more cattle than any other individual.

While Goodnight and Chisum were alike with reference to their daring, and their fundamental knowledge of the cattle industry, they were opposite in character. Goodnight was aggressive in all his undertakings and always ready to experiment with some new venture. Chisum was willing to settle down upon his huge ranch and take life as it came and be content with the natural increase from his herds. Both were courageous men, but Goodnight was a fighter, while Chisum was a pacifist, who avoided trouble whenever possible. While Goodnight credited him with being the best trail man of that time, Chisum did not attempt to exploit this ability. It is said that during his entire career, where danger stalked him at every turn, there were only a few occasions when he felt the need of going armed.

Although it seemed that Chisum desired only to live in peace and enjoy the fruits of his labor and management, he was not permitted to do so. From the outset his cattle were subjected to raids by marauding Indians and later by organized bands of cattle thieves. Through a combination of unfortunate circumstances he became deeply involved in the Lincoln County war which terrorized southeastern New Mexico for a decade. Through it all he rode the highways and walked the streets of Lincoln and Fort Sumner alone and unattended, as fearlessly as though he were moving about in a peaceful eastern village.

If Chisum was a pacifist, it was not so with the men he carried upon his pay roll. They committed themselves to his interests with a loyalty that is the finest trait of human nature and protected his property with their guns and their lives. His own closest call to violent death was no doubt when the outlaw William Bonney, better known as Billy the Kid, threatened to kill him at the termination of their relationship. Why the threat was not carried out is still an unexplained mystery. The Kid was not given to idle talk and another murder charged to his bloody career meant nothing to him at all.

The Lincoln County war was a unique chapter in range cattle history. It raged over all southeastern New Mexico, but centered around the towns of Lincoln and Fort Sumner. It lasted for many years and exceeded in violence any other factional disturbance the country ever knew. It was carried on by two sets of the most desperate hired killers that ever arrayed themselves against one another. Much has been written about events which led up to the bloody epoch, and it would require an entire volume to recount all the details. It is sufficient to say that John Chisum felt impelled to finance one side of the feud which placed him and Billy the Kid together. Up to this time, the Kid was considered to be an inoffensive orphan waif only sixteen years of age.

The disturbance had been brewing for some time because of raids Chisum's enemies were making against his cattle. It burst into flame when a group of killers murdered a harmless man who was a friend and partner of Chisum's, and who had also gained the worshipful adoration of the Kid by his benevolence toward a homeless boy. Stricken with grief at the untimely death of his benefactor, the Kid took matters in his own hands and sought to even the score by killing two of the murderers. Since this group was already aligned against Chisum, they retaliated by making a raid upon the Chisum cattle in which one of his cowboys was killed. The only course left open for him now was to hire a corresponding bunch of gunmen to protect his own interests, and Billy the Kid was included among them. When the leader of the Chisum forces was killed during a battle, the Kid's exploits had been so daring and effective that he graduated to leadership as a matter of course. The war raged until the death of the man behind the anti-Chisum forces, which came about from natural causes. This event automatically stopped the pay of one faction and with nothing else to be gained by continuing the hostilities, Chisum was glad to withdraw financial support from his own side, which had become quite a burden. This is what precipitated the misunderstanding between him and the Kid when his life was threatened.

Withdrawal of financial backing from both sides failed to stop the war, however. Deep fears and hatreds had been created, and the disturbance ran on and on until most of the partici-pants had died at the hands of one another. When finances ran low, time was taken out by both sides to engage in a little cattle stealing, or bank robbing to replenish empty pockets. Through it all swaggered Billy the Kid, with more individual killings to his credit than any other living man. The longer he operated, the more desperate and bloodthirsty he became, and he seemed to lead a charmed life. Twice he was captured and managed to escape by killing his guards. He ran loose and unfettered up and down the Pecos for years until he was finally stopped by that famous manhunter Pat Garrett, who bored a hole through his right side one night in a Mexican adobe house.

All through the war, Chisum kept himself in the clear. No charge of murder or complicity of murder was ever laid against him. None of his regular cowboys took an active part in the dis-turbances outside their own range lines, but there were times when the battle was brought to them, by raids of their enemies upon the Jingle Bob cattle.

Like many others who led the way and laid the foundation of the cattle business at the risk of life, Chisum failed to adapt him-self to changing conditions. Before he died, he saw the immense fortune he had created dwindle to almost nothing in compari-son. Most of the great domain where his cattle grazed up and down the Pecos for a hundred miles and as far back from water as they could range, fell into the hands of others, and Chisum's properties shrank to a pitiful holding.

The average person will not be concerned with the causes which led up to Chisum's financial failure. Nevertheless the name of John Chisum is entitled to its well-earned place in cattle his-tory. He established the first large ranch the country ever knew; he trod where others feared to follow; and he played an active part in opening up one of the most desirable territories for cattle production in the entire country.

CHAPTER SEVEN

ON TO THE GREAT
NORTHWEST

Like any new and unproven project, the cattle business was developed by the process of trial and error. At no time in history had large herds of wild cattle been handled in such a manner. The first Texas drovers were unfamiliar with the art of cowherding and they had learned the hard way. There was no book of rules to serve as a guide. Proof of their lack of knowledge was the selection of the perilous and impossible routes through the Ozark Mountains for their first drives, but it did not take them long to learn. Those first few years of groping blindly in the darkness taught them many things, one of which was that cattle could live through the winter of a cold country.

When the Kansas markets first opened up, it was the general opinion that no animal could survive the northern winters without shelter from storms and a supplement of feed that had been previously prepared. They had a fair example of Nature's works before them as a foundation for such belief. The great herds of buffalo that ranged what was later to become the cattle kingdom of the world drifted back and forth from north to south with the change of seasons. In addition, many Indians made seasonal migrations, while others sought out the most sheltered terrain for their winter camps, and kept their ponies alive by pulling grass for them during the summer and preserving it as a cured hay for winter. If the Indian ponies and the hardy buffalo could not survive, there was no reason at all to believe that a cow raised in the warm climes of Texas could live through the northern winters.

Inclusion of the northern ranges into bonafide beef-producing areas came about in a peculiar manner. No doubt the first animals to winter in these regions were work oxen and a few milch cows belonging to emigrants crossing the Great Plains, who for one reason or another became stranded and were forced to tie up for the winter while en route. It was found that these animals withstood the winter remarkably well, but this fact did not prove the feasibility of wintering large herds upon the ranges. With only a few gentle animals to care for, the owners could easily find adequate shelter for them behind a cut bank during a storm and aid them in securing food by scraping snow from the grass. To give a large herd such care would have been impossible.

Like many other elements of the cattle industry, this knowledge was acquired more by accident than by design. It is said that a Texas drover arrived at the shipping point in Kansas with his cattle in such poor condition that he could not sell them. He had made a late start and encountered a bad season on the trail, with great deluges of rainfall dogging him all the way. The grass grew rank and slushy, and his animals lost flesh instead of gaining. High water in the streams he had to cross delayed him even more, and when he arrived, there was no demand for any cattle unfit for slaughter. Neither was there enough time before winter for him to fatten them upon the range nearby. No speculator would think of investing in a herd to hold and winter upon the Kansas range. There was nothing left for the drover to do but make the best out of a bad situation and attempt to winter them himself.

Thinking he was ruined financially, but not willing to give up without a trial, he prepared to go into winter quarters. He spent some time in scouting out the country to locate a favorable place. He selected a locality some thirty or forty miles west of Abilene between the Solomon and Smoky Hill rivers. There was an abundance of grass in the wide valleys between the two streams, and the ridge of hills on both sides gave promise of a little shelter. He threw his herd back into this ideal spot and, hoping for the best, turned them loose. Knowing that cattle would be inclined to drift south before the storms just as the buffalo did, he divided his men and horses into small groups and established line camps along the divide south of the Smoky Hill.

To his surprise, those cattle continued to gain in flesh after the first freezes and snowstorms struck. He discovered that the short buffalo grass had cured to an exact state of perfection, and that it possessed strength and nutritious qualities almost unbelievable. Before the winter was over, he saw them with enough strength to wade through deep snowdrifts searching out uncovered feed in sheltered places, or upon hillsides where the wind had whipped certain spots bare of snow. He found that his saddle horses, which were jaded from the long and hard trip up the trail and decimated in flesh from subsisting on the slushy grass of the summer rains, took on added strength and were able to carry their riders up and down the line. Those Texas cow ponies had never seen a snowdrift in their lives; yet, he saw their instinctive nature assert itself when they uncovered grass to eat by pawing the snow away just as their ancestors had done on the steppes of Russia thousands of years before.

It is true that these warm-blooded animals from the south did drift before the storms, but it was not difficult for the line riders to overtake and return them to the winter grounds. To the owner's surprise those cattle came through the dreaded Kansas winter in better shape than when they had started into it. With the coming of spring, and the new crop of grass, they improved in flesh remarkably fast, and before the first drives began to arrive from Texas, they were fat and ready for market. It was fortunate that this particular drover struck a mild winter. There have been other winters when the death losses in this region were enormous and devastating. Cattlemen learned this in later years, but they found that severe winters were far enough apart that the average benefits over a period of years justified them in taking the risk.

Now this drover had another pleasant surprise awaiting him. The animals that made up this herd were aged steers and, according to all knowledge, they had arrived at a maturity of growth. In spite of this common belief, he found that the northern winter and the wonderful grass of the Kansas prairie had worked another miracle. Those aged steers continued to grow and spread out during the next spring and summer, and they went to market weighing two hundred pounds more than the same class of cattle arriving from Texas that year; they commanded, as well, a higher price by the pound. Thus it was learned purely by accident not only that Texas cattle could stand the northern winter, but also that they made an added growth and improved in quality while doing it.

Other trail men took advantage of this knowledge, which made them all more independent. From this time on, no more cattle were sacrificed to unscrupulous buyers, who had, in previous times, used the threat of the northern winters to beat the price down when the market became congested. If the price was not suitable now, the cowman simply threw his herd back to some favorable spot, and carried it through the winter by loose herding and line riding. With the knowledge that cattle could stand the northern winters and that the sojourn also improved them, the cowman brought immense areas of hitherto untouched and virgin range land within his scope.

There is still a question as to the exact time a cowman drove his herd to the extreme north with the express intention of wintering it there. Certainly no movement of any proportion to stock the northern ranges was under way before the middle, or late, Seventies. The first drives to find their way to the northern countries were for the purpose of sale and slaughter. Before the Abilene and Ellsworth markets were firmly established, both Charles Goodnight and John Chisum were stringing their herds across the divide to the Pecos River and into New Mexico. While Chisum, without question, was hunting free and open range and plenty of it with the intention of starting a ranch, the place of his location in southern New Mexico could hardly be called the north. While, on the other hand, Goodnight's operations led him into Colorado and southern Wyoming, his first drives to these regions were solely for the purpose of selling beef cattle to the mining camps in the mountains. His branching out into the ranching business in this country was a result of these earlier ventures.

The first recorded drive to the extreme north was a herd moving out of Texas in 1866. Like all other early ones, it was solely for the purpose of sale. A young and adventurous speculator from Illinois had dipped into Texas and bought a herd of cattle for the Kansas trade. Finding market conditions at the railhead unsatisfactory, the owner turned northwest, and started on the long trek to the mining camps around Bozeman, Montana. He drifted up the Smoky Hill; thence across to the Republican and the North Platte to the Yellowstone, and on to destination. There is sharp disagreement as to the number of cattle included in this movement. The accounts vary from two hundred fifty to a thousand head. In all probability it was the smaller number — or even less. Without intention to dispute the truthfulness of the story or to detract from the glory of the achievement, the writer believes it would have been impossible to manage a herd of sizable numbers under conditions existing at that time.

The account tells of difficulties encountered and of hardships endured during the trip, which can be readily believed. The wonder of it all is that any of those engaged in the undertaking (or their stock) came out alive. The story tells of passing through Wyoming and into Montana in the dead of winter. It tells of skirmishes with roving bands of hostile Indian tribes, and of how the outfit was held up indefinitely at Fort Phil Kearney by military authorities for fear the entire crew of men would be massacred by the Indians. After becoming fretful at the delay and restraint imposed upon them by the Army, the drovers eventually stole away with their herd and continued the trip without mishap. It would be a safe venture to say that no large herd of wild cattle was ever handled in such a manner.

In the first place, winter in that region, with its sub-zero temperatures and sweeping blizzards, is not a pleasant and simple event. It was only when grass and water were available in abundance and when the drive was under skilled management that a large herd could be moved over a long distance and kept in thriving condition. Certainly it could not have been done during a northern winter. Cattle will drift before a severe storm, regardless of the efforts and determination of men who might try to hold them. There is no way on a wide open prairie to overcome the forces of nature and the instinctive actions of animals.

Old time cowboys who rode the winter lines of long ago know that it was extremely difficult to return a bunch of cattle forty or fifty miles to the home range after a storm — much less hold them while one was raging. Neither could the cattle have lived through the ordeal. While it had been proven that cattle could winter in a northern country, they could not do so with the restrictions of being constantly under herd imposed upon them. Neither could the men and horses have stood the hardships of being out in the weather with a herd both day and night under such circumstances. No doubt the drive was made, but it was bound to have been a very small herd indeed, and even so, it was a miracle that the undertaking was successful.

As has been stated, Dodge City was the last big shipping point for the Eastern market, but it was to remain a cowtown for many years to come. It sat squarely upon the main trail to the Northwest, and hundreds of thousands of cattle on their way to the northern ranges passed within sight of its buildings. It was the first trading point north of the Texas border, and all passing outfits pulled their wagons into town to replenish the supply of provisions. Here the cowboys turned in for a fling at hilarious celebration as a diversion for the lonely existence of trail monotony. Here the guns of the town marshals blazed in their determination to enforce law and order, and here the gamblers and painted women continued to ply their trades.

While the number of cattle driven to Kansas points and shipped to Eastern markets reached enormous proportions, it was hardly a beginning for the movement that was now under way. The cattlemen had learned the value of the northern country for the growth and development of beef cattle, and the doors of a new world were wide open to them. The vast areas of grassland in all the states between the Rocky Mountains and the Missouri River were ready for inclusion in the cattlemen's kingdom, and they were not long in taking advantage of the opening. Soon the herds were pounding northward.

It is difficult to believe that such enormous numbers of cattle could have been driven from a single state in the course of three decades without depleting the entire supply, but such was the case. After a careful analysis, it is understandable. The cattle-breeding portion of Texas embraced large areas, and the number of animals on hand at the beginning was staggering. When the drives first started, the ranges were literally crawling alive with them. Steers ranged in age up to ten and twelve years, and these were the first ones to go. Grown steer cattle were the only class that was marketable at that time; therefore, disposition of these animals in no way retarded reproduction. In fact, removal of the surplus from the country served to stimulate and increase production. This lightened up the already over-burdened range. With more and better feed available, the mother cows, which were always the first to perish from feed shortage, were much better fed and the winter death loss among them was greatly curtailed.

On the other hand, younger animals were the most desirable for stocking distant ranges, since it was expected to hold them for at least two years for growth and development. This transitory movement was confined to steer cattle, for it was common knowledge that a mother cow, after having her strength drained away all summer by a suckling calf, could not live through a severe winter without a supplement of prepared tame feed, which was not available at that time.

Here we find the cattle industry emerging into a new phase. There were future planning and arrangements being made to hold a certain class of animals over a period of time for better growth and development. The cost of driving these cattle to their new ranges and holding them until fully matured was comparatively low, while the prospects of profits were large. The excellent quality of the grass, combined with the northern winters, had a miraculous effect. Even an aged animal that had reached its full growth in Texas spread out and took on added weight after a winter in the north.

While all states comprising the Great Plains area were more or less adaptable for stock growing, Montana and parts of the Dakotas in the days of free and open range proved to be the most favorable. Cold weather and winter storms were the most dreaded elements of the northern country, and it is odd that the two northernmost states should hold the least risks for winter losses. There is a good reason for such a condition. The topographical lay of the land makes it so. The country varies from rolling prairies to rough breaks, and there are comparatively few stretches of flat plains in these regions. Adjacent to the open land are wide areas of Bad Lands which furnished excellent protection from biting winds of the blizzards that sweep down across the country. Cattle are less inclined to drift from sheltered places to become confused, and lost from water, and to wear away their strength in useless travel. Because of this country's broken surface and deep recesses, there was never a time when all feed was covered with snow. Numerous flowing springs of comparatively warm water scattered throughout the regions assured ample stock water when open drinking places in other areas were frozen solid by the extreme weather.

In those days the farther north cattle roamed the stronger and more nutritious the grasses seemed to be, and Montana grew the best that was ever known. Records of cattle sales at the stockyards, up to forty years ago, will show that prime Montana grass steers, bred in Texas and double wintered in the north, and that had never eaten a bite of tame feed in their lives, commanded top prices over all cattle. The range is grazed closer nowadays, and consequently the abundance of grass necessary for producing the highest quality beef no longer exists, but there was a time when northwestern range steers topped the price of animals from corn feed lots.

Courageous and heartbreaking attempts were made to incorporate the high and open steppes of central Canada into a grazing country, but as a large-scale range proposition, it was a failure.

Summer conditions were ideal, but winters were far too severe. Cattlemen learned to their sorrow from heavy death losses that the wide-open and unprotected regions of the far north were not adaptable to such an undertaking. Since the herds have been cut down to smaller numbers, and the necessity of preparing tame feed and shelter for the winter is recognized, Canada has turned out to be a profitable stock-farming country.

This does not mean to imply that Montana was the only Northern state favorable for stock growing. In fact some may dispute that it was best fitted for open-range operations in the early days. Before Montana was ever stocked, the flow of cattle was spreading over western Kansas, eastern Colorado, Nebraska and Wyoming. Cattle were going west to Arizona and California, but these movements never reached sizable proportions. The two latter states were used for breeding grounds the same as Texas, and within a few years cattle were being exported from them.

To the states making up the Great Plains went the big drives. From the late Seventies to almost the turn of the century, monstrous herds were continually on the trail during the spring and summer months. Since the supply had to be renewed approximately every two years to fill the place vacated by those shipped out to market, the total number reached enormous proportions. While the railroads had built across the country east and west and shut off the Kansas Trail, even to this day there is but one line traversing the cattle country that could be called a north and south road, and it is not a direct route by any means.

Thus, on to the Northwest the great herds moved. While the trails to the Kansas market remained open for some eight or ten years, the one north and south was open for thirty. During that time the heaviest movement of cattle overland from one part of the country to another the world has ever known took place. It was then that the profession of trail driving reached its climax, and geniuses of the trade were developed to hold the spotlight of the era.

The names of McCoy the promoter, John Chisum, the rancher, and Charles Goodnight, the foremost leader of them all, have crept into the record. Now the time has come to name John Blocker, the most sanguine trail man the world has ever known. From an humble and a modest beginning, John Blocker engaged in the cattle business while still in his teens. He was too young to take part in the pioneering stage of the industry, but before he had finished his work, his name became a symbol wherever cattle were herded together. Fired by the ambition of youth and by confidence in his own ability, he lived to see the time when his Block R brand was known from the Rio Grande to the Canadian border. He was also one of the most expert ropers who ever threw a lariat, and for years his name was synonymous with a loop. Around the turn of the century it was a common thing to hear a cowboy anywhere between the Yellowstone and the Pecos remark that he "spread his Blocker." The phrase became as widely used as the famous *da le vuelta*.

John Blocker was not a great rancher by any means. While he operated ranches at both ends of the trail, he was mainly a trader who would either buy or sell — according to the dictates of his own judgment. He never raised more than a fraction of the animals he drove, but the number of cattle that passed through his hands would rank close to those handled by Charles Goodnight. There was a time when the campfires of his trail outfits blazed at intervals of seventy-five or a hundred miles, all the way between Texas and Montana, in a single night. It is said that he had eighty thousand cattle on the trail during one season. Such an undertaking would require at least twenty-five outfits, with a personnel of two hundred fifty men and twenty-five hundred horses. Like the promoter Joe McCoy, and the rancher Chisum, and the pioneer Charles Goodnight, he lived to see the fortune he had wrung from the many trail drives crumble to a fraction of what is was at one time. Regardless of the finish, his name is emblazoned upon the pillar of cattle history, never to be erased.

The trail from the breeding grounds of Texas to the northern ranges was a long and arduous one, with its elements of danger. On the other hand, there was the lure of fascinating glamor and adventure to induce a cowboy to make the trip. There was the suggestion of romance in the landmarks and stations along the way, such as the Canadian, the Smoky Hill, the Platte, the Powder and Yellowstone rivers. There were the towns of Dodge City, Ogallala, Julesburg, Deadwood and Cheyenne, each with its highlights of history and tragedies. Then at the end of the cowboys' reign, came Miles City on the Yellowstone, which was the last to become sophisticated and up to date.

Montana! There was magic and romance in the name. The lure drew many a Texas cowboy across the plains, and hills, and rivers, two thousand miles from home. It was in Montana that the long trail ended and the gigantic cow outfits came into being. It was here that cowpunching reached it grand climax, and it was here that the cowboy made his last stand before romance and glamor faded from the calling. From down on the Rio Grande and Gulf Coast regions the romantic era had started, and it ended along the Canadian border.

And Texas! Grand old Texas! She played a grand role in the creation and finishing of the great period. In the faraway Northwest, another jewel was added to her already flaming crown of the five-pointed star. She wrote her name upon the final pages of open-range cattle history by the class of men she sent north with her herds. In a later chapter it will be shown why no weak, timid, or unfit man could exist among those resolute and self-willed individuals who made up that grand array of hard-riding, hilarious men of the cattle country. Since driving the great herds two thousand miles away through an unknown land was filled with more or less of uncertainties and danger, it was only natural that it would attract the most daring from among the groups of daring men.

Not all of those who traveled to the northland were good men as measured by standards of right and wrong. Many of them would hardly be considered proper models after whom a young boy might pattern his life. Some of the most desperate and quick-triggered characters who ever squinted through a gunsight helped to make up that array of picturesque individuals who followed the herds over long miles of trail from the Gulf to the Canadian border. There was a good reason for it too. By the time the northern trails were well opened up, some law and order had come to the southern countries. Many a daring bank hold-up, or train robber, or notorious horse and cattle thief found things too hot for comfort in the homeland and sought wider and safer fields of operation. But good or bad, they knew the intricacies of cowpunching, and none of them was a coward. By their knowledge and daring, those first trail drivers established a reputation for Texas men that has remained unchanged.

Among the thousands who made the trips, many of them stayed to exert further influence upon the lore and history of the country. Even today, it is not uncommon to hear the soft accent of the Texas drawl along the Yellowstone or the Powder, spoken by a native son who has never lived south of the Wyoming line. There is also a Spanish flavor to the language adopted many years ago from the Mexican vaqueros, which has clung to the cattle trade from one end of cattledom to the other. The familiar word "rodeo" is Spanish for roundup, and at one time it was used for just what it means. Gatherings where cowboys met to exhibit and contest their skill with one another were called cowboys' reunions, and they were free from the professional aspect, as we know of rodeos today. "Corral" means a pen, or small enclosure for holding stock; "remuda" stands for a bunch of saddle horses; along with the contraction of *la reata* into the word lariat and the widely used phrase of *da le vuelta*. Many Spanish words are still in general use, while many have been discarded and forgotten. Others have been butchered so badly that their coiner would not know his own creations if he met them in the middle of the road.

It was universally recognized that a Texas man was the most expert of all cowhands. For years the word had its magical effect on the great cattle country of the Northwest. It was an open sesame for a cowboy seeking a job. By the time the Northwest trail was in full operation, the knack of handling cattle had reached a scientific state, and the Texas men were in possession of all the knowledge. They had learned what the Mexican vaquero knew and added much wisdom of their own. Foremen, or wagon bosses as they were called, who supervised the operation of the outfits were Texas men themselves and they knew their fellow men's ability. Time and trial had proven them masters at their trade and their reputation of courage and loyalty was beyond question. After others had a chance to learn the trade, many of them ranked along with the Texans, but in the early days, the men from the south held the edge.

As an illustration of the weight the name carried at one time, it is fitting to relate a true incident of human interest that happened in those grand and glorious days. An Iowa farm boy, with plenty of courage but little else to fit him for a cowboy's role, had ventured out in the land of great romance. At a pre-roundup meeting he had gone from one wagon boss to another in a vain quest for a job. One look at his innocent face and imitation regalia would suffice to betray his background, but the refusal would seldom come without first ascertaining his origin. Finally a veteran cowhand, out of pity for the discouraged boy, gave him some useful advice.

"Go hit that man up there for a job," he said, pointing out a wagon boss who had just emerged from a saloon and was standing upon the sidewalk. "Tell him you're from Texas — and he'll put you to work."

Undaunted, the Iowa boy acted upon this suggestion.

"Where're you from?" was the first question his prospective employer asked him.

"I'm from Texas," the Iowa lad answered bravely.

"What part of Texas do you all hail from?" was the next question.

This caught the boy unawares, and he dropped his eyes, while he hesitated. "I'm from Texas River," he hedged.

The wagon boss stood straight and rigid, looking into the hopeful and upturned face of the farm boy. He let his eyes run over the aspirant's dress, and noted the new checkered shirt open at the collar; the loud-colored bandana knotted around his neck, with creases where it had lain folded upon the store counter. His gaze ranged downward to the hand-me-down boots, with not a stirrup leather rub upon the legs nor a spur mark upon the heels. The contempt that a straightforward and truthful man has for a deceitful liar was in evidence upon the foreman's face.

"You Texas River so-and-sos are too tough for me," he said disgustedly.

Beads of sweat mingled with the down upon the farm boy's upper lip. His blue eyes were filled with anxious hope, while he withstood that withering glare of the one he considered high and mighty. At the foreman's sarcastic verdict, he dropped his eyes and something akin to a sob escaped his lips. Then came a sudden switch to the little drama that was almost a case of life and death to the unsophisticated boy. The sternness of the wagon boss's face relaxed and a humorous twinkle came into his eyes. A ghost of a smile played around his mouth while he placed his hand affectionately upon the boy's shoulder.

"You Texas River so-and-sos are tough all right — but I've got a tough outfit too — and I guess we can stand you."

The above incident furnishes an insight into the character of those hard-bitten cowmen who were not without a tender streak in their makeup. A beautiful sequel to this story can be told, and an example of human gratitude displayed.

From the moment that self-confident wagon boss laid his hand upon the boy's shoulder, he became the object of hero worship. In this travail of human endeavor, some men go up while others go down. The innocent farm boy lived to reach the station of financial and public success, while the idol of his young manhood sank to a low level of society. Regardless of his misfortune, the once proud wagon boss always retained one champion in the leading financier and mayor of the town.

Yes, indeed, the Texas cowboy entered into a new era when he found himself in Montana. Many things were the same, but many were different. Although he handled the same cattle, rode the same horses, and worked very much with the same men, conditions were not the same as they were at home. His wages were almost doubled; and compared to the poorly equipped outfits he had followed in Texas, the present layouts were almost a paradise. No penurious and miserly standards could ever be laid to the early Northern cow outfits. They furnished their men with the best food and living standards that could be used expediently, regardless of cost.

In Texas, all cooking was done over an open fire, hot or cold, rain or shine; meals in Montana were prepared upon a range stove under shelter of a tent. There was no more standing around a smoldering campfire with smoke searing one's eyes while trying to dry out water-soaked clothing. There was no more sleeping out upon wet ground during a pouring rain in a bed that was soaking wet to begin with. There were no more days and nights without a cup of steaming coffee to warm one's insides when rain was too heavy for an open fire to burn. The outfits of the Northwest eliminated many hardships of a cowboy's life.

The cook tent was an arrangement with walls high enough for a man to stand without his head striking the top. One half was devoted exclusively to the cook and horse wrangler; here their beds were spread and the cooking was done. There was also space allotted for a pile of wood to dry out during wet weather. The other side was used as sleeping space for cowboys, and there was room enough for six or eight men and their beds. In addition to the cook tent, there were canvas teepees accommodating two beds easily, where other men paired off. It was only in cases of extreme shelter shortage that two men slept together. Each cowboy had his own bed, and he slept in it alone. With the cook tent and the sleeping tents raised, and with some three hundred or more saddle horses grazing nearby; with some twenty or thirty riders in evidence with a herd of cattle in the background; and the bed and chuck wagons amidst the setting, a Northwestern cow outfit in camp was an impressive sight indeed.

The food was the best that could be had under the circumstances. Outside of fresh vegetables and dairy products, nothing was lacking. Those old roundup cooks were past masters in the preparation of food, and they took deep pride in their calling. As in any other good meal, then, as now, meat was the main item on the menu. On the roundups the choicest cuts of beef were always available. The cowboys did their own slaughtering and dressing with an unlimited number of animals from which to make their selection. As a diversion, an adequate amount of cured meats processed in packing houses was always on hand, but no bonafide cowboy ever admitted that there was a substitute for range-killed and dressed beef. As a substitute for the lack of fresh-grown food, a supply of canned fruits and vegetables was on hand. Baking powder, or sourdough biscuits fresh and hot from the oven constituted the bread portion of the meals. Besides the staples with which to work, those cooks had means of preparing some tasty dishes with by-products of a young beef furnishing the main ingredients, such as the brains, liver, sweetbreads and chitterlings.

While the Texas cowboy in the Northwest found his standard of living greatly improved and his wages greatly increased, he still lived in a familiar environment. He found gamblers, saloon keepers and painted women on hand to take his money the same as they had done in Abilene, Ellsworth, Newton and Dodge City. His hours of work were just as exacting and perhaps longer than heretofore. No set of men ever hit the line harder and remained on the job longer than those Montana roundup hands. A working day was not determined by fixed hours, but it ran around the clock, from daylight to darkness, with a part of the night thrown in for good measure, while the hands stood guard around the herd. The wrangler had the saddle horses in the rope corral well before daylight, and before sunup, the outfit was on the move. During those long summer days in the Northwest range country, when the sun was at its zenith, a cowboy's period of rest was very short indeed.

But all good things must eventually come to an end. In time, encroachment of the farmer into the virgin range land had its effect. The trail running through Dodge City, Ogallala and Julesburg to Montana was finally closed. The Goodnight and Loving Trail up through New Mexico, over Trinchera Pass into Colorado, and thence to Wyoming and Montana lasted for awhile longer but the end to it came in a few short years. The latter trail to the ranges of Dakota and Montana was not as widely used as the other. It drew only cattle from New Mexico and the Staked Plains area of Texas.

Sensing the trend of affairs, a few cattlemen set a move on foot to secure a right of way from the northern boundary of Texas to the grazing areas that were still unhampered by settlers. It was a gigantic and visionary undertaking, but it would have been a practical solution for the problem at that time. Extensive discussions of the proposal were carried on, and various meetings of interested parties were held, but the movement died away. Cattlemen were the most outstanding and outspoken individualists the world has ever known, and because of strong and divergent opinions they could not all agree. The project would have required a strip of land at least three miles wide and fifteen hundred miles in length. Because of the location of water, it could not have run in a straight line. In the light of present events, it is a pity that the proposal was not consummated. What a monument to that romantic era of American history it would be today.

The overland trails to the Northwest were closed long before the heavy movement of cattle ended. The railroads had pushed out through the cattle country and were in full operation before the farmers blocked the cattle trail. While the movement by rail was a roundabout and costly mode of transportation, it was employed extensively. By that time the great ranches that had been form-ing in Texas were well organized; they had not overlooked the advantage of maturing their products in the Northern ranges, and most of them established ranches there. It was found to be best to locate the young cattle in the North during the spring and early summer so they could acclimate themselves to the country before winter set in. Thus, for thirty days each spring, around the shipping points in Texas and New Mexico, there was a general congestion of cattle while great herds held out, waiting for their own turn at loading. For thirty days each spring loading crews worked day and night while solid trainloads of cattle pulled out toward the faraway destination.

As previously stated, the supply of cattle in the Northwest had to be renewed at least every two years. For many years it was thought that a mother cow could not live through the cold winters of that region. In time it was discovered that with a little assistance from supplemental feeds, a cow could live quite well and raise a calf at the same time. Thus the Northwest became a breeding ground as well as one for finishing. Broad valleys of the Platte, the Powder, the Yellowstone, the Missouri and hundreds of tributary streams abounded with great meadows of native grasses. The valley grass grew to considerable height in contrast to the short buffalo grass of the prairies, and when cut and cured, it made a most nourishing feed. Therefore, it was not long until the clatter of the mowing machine and creak of the hay stacker broke the stillness in primitive regions where previously the only sound made by a vehicle or machinery was the scratch of the Indian travois or the rattle of a roundup chuck wagon.

The mowing machine and its contemporary devices might well be charged as the beginning of the cowboy's end. Heretofore, he had shunned manual labor as though it were a pestilence. He considered it degrading to a man of his station who did his best work on horseback. He ranked a farmer on equality with the despised sheepherder. He never objected to the violent physical exertions required while branding stock; nor the long and grueling hours in the saddle in severe weather while riding wild and dangerous horses in between. He was even willing, and sometimes eager, to risk his life at gunfighting in the interest of his employer, but he drew the line at farming. Most of them refused point-blank to have any truck with such lowly degrading work, and, for some time, a cowman who wished to preserve winter hay was forced to recruit his hay hands from another source. Like all forces of progression, in time the objections to ranch work were worn away. Nowadays it is a common thing to see a champion rider or roper of the rodeos riding a mowing machine or pitching hay during an off season.

This does not mean that the practice of winter feeding set the cowboy adrift all at once. The haying season came at a time when roundup work was at its height, and for many years to come there was elbow room for a first-class cowhand to circulate around and display the arts of his trade. This was just a phase of the industry that marked the beginning of the end of romance and glamor. The decline was gradual, and it took years to reach its present status. In fact, the calling still seems to retain some of its lure and attracts many followers who appear to be well satisfied with their lot. The present setup and modes of operation would be very unattractive indeed to the old time cowhand.

In the meantime, small operators had been taking hold in the Northwest and establishing ranches. Many old time cowhands could see the handwriting upon the wall and concluded that if they had to degrade themselves with manual labor, they had just as well get into business for themselves and reap all the profits. Land laws governing the public domain operated in their favor. A prospective small cowman could file upon a piece of well-watered land for his homestead and start a small bunch of cattle while still drawing wages from a cow outfit. For awhile this practice was tolerated and even encouraged by the bigger outfits. It was a source of satisfaction to know that a loyal man was located within the confines of their range. In later years, when rustling of mavericks became too general and widespread, the proceeding was frowned upon, but there was no means of preventing it. The flow of small men was coming and it could not be stopped. This doomed the large-scale, open-range operations of the industry.

Certainly the period between the early Eighties and the turn of the century was the golden era for the cowman. He had all the range at his command that could be desired. It was during this time that large fortunes were made. To be sure, there were financial depressions and panics and drought conditions that in some cases swept fortunes away, but in the main, the cowman was on the ascendancy. Credit was easy and a reputable man could always find backing to start in business or recoup any losses.

Before the turn of the century, the cowman of the great Northwest felt the pinch of crowded range. The onward march of the homesteader was as relentless as the flow of a great river, and wrote the doom for the big outfits. Heretofore they had maintained a gentleman's agreement to respect each other's imaginary range lines, but there was no way to stop the homesteader and former cowboy who went into business on a small scale. For a short time the working cowboy was granted a longer lease on existence by the formation of pool outfits by the smaller operators, but that soon expired. Each individual learned to give his stock better care at all times during the year, which consideration made them less inclined to stray from home. Where in the old days cattle drifted before winter storms for a hundred miles or more, it came to be that instead of drifting away when a storm struck, the animals came to the home ranch, where they had learned that life-saving hay and other supplemental feed awaited them. Thus, in a last and final stand in the Northwest ranges, the open-range cowhand passed into oblivion, but his deeds and achievements will live forever in the memory of those who knew him.

CHAPTER EIGHT
BARBED WIRE
AND WINDMILLS

I N THE DECADE between the Seventies and the Eighties, two instruments were in the process of perfection which were to play a vital and lasting part with the cowman and his affairs. They were both distantly remote from the scene; and at the time of their creation, there is no reason to believe that either of the inventors ever dreamed of the grand scale upon which they were to be employed.

One was the invention of barbed wire, which gave the world its first and only cheap and practical fencing material. The other was the construction of the windmill. The deep-well machine had been perfected long ago, but from the standpoint of a cowman and his needs, it was useless without a contemporary device to bring water in sizable amounts, at a reasonable cost, to the earth's surface from deep underground.

The manufacture and sale of barbed wire in large quantities allowed the cowman to segregate his own stock from others and improve the blood strains according to his own ideas. The combination of the deep well and windmill brought millions of hitherto unused acres into the cowman's domain. These wide areas of unclaimed lands of the High Plains were the last to be invaded by the hungry cows that had now spread from the Gulf Coast to the Canadian border.

Fencing in America is an old institution. The first fences were erected by farmers in Virginia for the purpose of turning stock away from growing crops, but they were crude and expensive affairs indeed. They were constructed from split poles; the panels zigzagged and interlocked with each other in such a manner as to give the line stability. They were known as the stake-and-rider variety. Even though timber was abundantly plentiful, and wages were extremely low, the immense cost of such structures limited the enclosures to very small tracts. In the rockbound country of New England, stone fences were common, but the cost of erection restricted their general use. Indeed, the first settlers in Texas employed both of the above methods of enclosing small tracts of land, but they were for the purpose of keeping straying animals out of fields instead of holding large herds within.

As the tide of immigration from the Atlantic seaboard spread westward, the old style methods of fencing were retained.

When the crest reached the prairie regions of Illinois, Missouri, Iowa and Wisconsin, where there was neither rock nor timber in quantity, the settlers found themselves without adequate fencing material. It was these people who combined the grazing of a limited number of cattle with farming operations who first felt the imperative need of cheap fencing, instead of range cattlemen in the Far West. It was small stock farmers who carried on the experiments and who, after a few years of devoted thought and effort, arrived at a solution of the problem.

Board lumber freighted from distant sawmills and nailed to upright posts received the first trials; but it was soon found that the cost of this material was entirely prohibitive. Someone came forward with the idea of planting hedgerows of quick-growing trees to serve as barriers between the field crops and grazing lands. This plan won immediate popularity and received general adoption. While the hedgerow was the first practical substitute for the old style methods of fencing at a cost within bounds of reason, there were many objections to it. First, the plants required years of growth before attaining adequate size to be of service. When once set, a hedge fence became a permanent fixture, as there was no way of moving it around from one land line to another. The principal fault of hedges was that they did not restrain breachy animals as intended. Gentle cattle became accustomed to walking through and over the rows of delicate plants during early growth, and they continued to do so after the trees reached a respectable size.

Thus, with the fallacy of the common hedge demonstrated, someone suggested that a thorny bush would be the answer. It was argued that nothing short of a thorn "capable of inflicting pain" would turn a hog or cow. The new idea called for a general program of re-planting and cultivation. This system also received universal adoption. The practice of hedge planting became so popular that the seeds and sprouts of thorn-bearing plants skyrocketed in price. Those located in or near timberland

and who were fortunate enough to have a growth of the desired plants within their reach, found a remunerative side line to their other engagements in selling seeds and sprouts of thorny trees to residents on the prairie. While many farmers were growing and nurturing the tender hedge plants, waiting patiently for the day when they would arrive at a mature growth, others were working toward a more practical answer.

From the accounts of early barbed-wire history, it appears that many hopeful inventors were devoting thought and energy to the same project at the same time. Principal activities seem to have been centered around the town of De Kalb, Illinois. Experiments were carried out by farmers, or by men interested in farming. Smooth wire had been available for a short time at a tremendous price, but tests had proved it inadequate for the same reason that the common hedge had failed. Gentle cattle refused to be restrained by anything short of an "instrument capable of inflicting pain" upon them during their moments of transgression. Thus, the would-be inventors devoted their efforts toward that end.

It was a farmer by name of John F. Glidden who made the first strand of barbed wire. This invention not only solved a needy and vexatious question of that day, but it also has stood the test of time. From the number of applications for patents filed immediately after the first public exhibition, it would appear that many of Glidden's neighbors had the same general idea. From the bitter and costly litigation that raged over a period of years before the question of patent rights was settled, one is led to believe that more or less of skulduggery had been going on. It is evident that others had either been spying upon Glidden during his work and experiments, or that, because of pride and self-esteem, he had bragged about his accomplishments to the extent that neighbors were kept informed of his progress, and later, some of them at least, violated his confidence.

The first barbed wire made by Glidden was turned out by a slow and laborious process. It was done by cutting short pieces of wire to serve as barbs, one at a time by hand, and then clamping them around a larger strand. He openly exhibited his first wire in 1873, and sold the first spool in 1874. It was at this time that trouble broke out in the home camp. Several of his former friends and acquaintances came forward with a similar product. In the end, Glidden's rights were confirmed by court action which left him with a virtual monopoly to manufacture and sell barbed wire.

The price of the first wire made in such a manner was so high that it was beyond the reach of the average farmer. Glidden succeeded in arousing the interest of an Eastern manufacturer from whom he had been buying his smooth wire for the newly created industry. A representative from the factory came out to look over his proposition and saw great possibilities in it, provided they could contrive to manufacture the wire cheaply and on a large scale. The upshot was that the factory perfected a machine for cutting the barbs and clamping them onto the strand which produced large quantities at a reasonable cost. Eventually the large single strand was discarded in favor of two smaller ones twisted together, with the barb clamped to one of them. That style of wire is in use to this day.

When the Eastern manufacturer started making barbed wire in large quantities, royalties from the sales made Glidden a rich man. Some authorities cite the abrupt decline in prices as proof of its popularity. In 1875 barbed wire sold for twenty dollars per hundred pounds. By 1880 the price was cut in half, and during the panic and money shortage days of 1897, it sold for less than two dollars per hundred. This was the lowest price barbed wire ever reached during its entire history.

At the beginning, barbed wire was very remote from the open range cattle industry. Up to the time Glidden was involved in the series of legal battles to protect his patent rights, it is doubtful if the range cattlemen west of the Missouri had ever heard of him or his product. Neither is there anything of record to show that he had the least perception of what he was about to start. His only thought was to create an instrument to turn cattle and other stock away from fields of growing crops, and he never dreamed that his wire would soon be used to enclose vast areas of grazing land situated hundreds of miles from a ploughed furrow. A wide gulf of distance and environment and customs separated the two localities, but barbed wire was destined to serve one as well as the other.

The custom of handling cattle in large numbers was growing into an art of high technique. Men were acquiring skill and developing a science of the trade day by day, while courageous and resourceful individuals were arising to heights of business success. The industry was gaining wide publicity both at home and abroad and attracting large volumes of capital, seeking grand returns upon investment. Combinations and corporations were being formed to embark upon gigantic business adventures, and the cowboy was rightfully and truly coming into his own. Stories of his deeds and exploits were being sung far and wide, laying the groundwork for his everlasting reputation. This was the situation when barbed wire edged into the cattle country to write its short and bloody chapter of history.

Those who first engaged in the cattle business had done so more or less from accident, or from dire necessity. Now, men were committing their life work to the calling, and laying plans for their sons to carry on after their incapacitation or demise. With that program in mind, many had bought land with the intention of making a permanent location. There is inherent among all peoples a longing first, to acquire land, and then to hold absolute jurisdiction over it. The Western cowman was no different from the average in this respect. In his case, it was a desire to run his own cattle upon his own land and keep the animals of other people off. Up to the time that barbed wire came upon the scene, it had not been possible to do so.

On the other hand, there was a stronger reason which influenced cattlemen in their desire to hold absolute jurisdiction over their land. Some had come to learn that it would pay them to improve the quality of their herds. During infrequent trips to the corn belt regions east of the Mississippi, they were brought in contact with farmers and cattle feeders of that area. They saw a more desirable class of stock than the Longhorns of the open range. There were Shorthorn and Durham herds that produced a heavier steer and a better grade of beef at three years of age than their Longhorns did at six. With the business knowledge they were gaining along with the cattle lore, it was a simple matter for them to figure out how much more profitable their undertaking would be if they could introduce the blood strains of those larger and better animals into their own native stock.

Until the early Eighties, there had been little change in the quality of cattle running upon the open range. Selective breeding had made some improvement, but it was barely noticeable. Progressive cowmen realized the need of cross breeding with a better-blooded class of cattle, but they were unable to perfect a suitable plan for such a program. No individual felt as though he could afford to furnish graded bulls for breeding purposes as long as all cattle mixed together without restraint. A movement was started with the purpose of bringing all cattlemen into an association to regulate the number and quality of bulls that were to be turned loose upon the range, but the proposal died before it got past the talking stage.

Cattlemen were such strong individualists that they never agreed upon any one question at a time. Few were willing to commit themselves to any kind of a program in which their own course of action might be governed by the will of another. Many argued that such a measure would necessitate telling publicly how many cattle each owned, and they considered that to be nobody's business — not even the tax assessor's; thus they would have nothing to do with such an arrangement. As a result, the few men who were determined to breed up their own herds in spite of handicaps were forced to limit their importation of graded bulls to a comparatively small number and to go to the extra expense of close-herding them with a bunch of selected cows. This was done to some extent, but with the adoption of fencing, the opportunity for herd improvement was open to all and at a cost within bounds of reason. Within a few years, large areas of land were being enclosed behind the shining strands of galvanized barbed wire.

The land laws of Texas were favorable to such an arrangement. Annexation agreements adopted when the Republic was admitted to the Union stipulated that the state would retain full sovereignty over all her public domain. Thus, the policy of selling large tracts of land, or leasing it for a term of years to cowmen, was adopted. In this manner great ranches were organized, and thousands of cattle in a single brand grazed upon blocks of land under the control of individuals. Thus, it was in Texas where the first big ranches were fenced, and it was there that improvement in the breeding of cattle on a large scale was first started.

If the land laws of Texas were favorable to fencing, such was not the case in other states and territories that made up the great open cattle ranges. These lands came under the strict laws of the Federal Government. They were designed solely for the benefit of homesteaders which prohibited anyone from enclosing an area larger than the legal homestead of less than a section. A few cow outfits ignored the law, but they lived to regret it. The Government not only forced them to gather up their fences and throw the country open again, but heavy fines were assessed against the transgressors for violation of the land laws. In later years when the Government despaired of the various Indian tribes making stock growers, the Bureau of Indian Affairs adopted the policy of leasing certain portions of Indian reservations to stockmen where fencing was permitted. Thus, in this manner, many famous ranches were established on Indian land, of which the most noteworthy were those located in the Oklahoma and Indian Territories, now comprising the state of

Oklahoma. The Oklahoma ranches were closed out in the latter part of the past century when the country was opened to the public for settlement, but much of the Indian land in the western part of the country was under lease to outsiders until comparatively recent times.

Soon after the manufacture of barbed wire reached quantity production, it found its way to the cattle ranges of Texas. Every means of transportation known in that day was employed. The wire came by ship from the Atlantic seaboard to Gulf Coast points. It moved by barges down the Mississippi to be transferred to the newly constructed railroads for shipment to the end of steel. From there it was freighted by horse, mule, and ox-drawn wagons deep into the interior where the large ranches lay sprawling. Fence posts were cut and hauled from the cedar brakes of the hill country, or made from native mesquite trees in the valleys. Before long, hundreds of miles of four-strand wires supported by sturdy posts stretched across hills and prairies.

The program of fencing the cattle ranges did not meet with unanimous approval by any means. Many men looked upon the project with disfavor and registered strong objections to it. Instead of having their range problems solved as they had hoped, the cow outfits found out they had let themselves in for some serious trouble. They had not taken into account the opposition of those who believed in free use of all public domain by all people as set out by the land laws of the Federal Government in other cattle states. Before the fencing project was fairly under way, solemn warning to stop it was received from unknown parties. When the warnings went unheeded, destructive measures were set in motion. Those opposed to fencing organized themselves into secret bands, and under cover of darkness many miles of the newly erected fences were cut down. The conflict threatened to become the most violent disturbance the country had known since the days of Reconstruction.

Although the fence cutters, as they came to be called, had no legal status to uphold them, there was a semblance of moral right and justice upon their side. Many of the cow outfits had become just as greedy and grasping as some men in other walks of life. They secured legal title to only scattering tracts of land, and now they attempted to grab much of the public domain in between by enclosing it all in the fenced area. This resulted in shutting out some small cowmen who could afford to buy but little land and who had always depended upon free range for their stock. In many cases they were left outside and cut off entirely from water by the fence lines. With disaster staring them in the face, they did not take it lying down.

The small operators, with their limited number of stock, were not alone in their protests. Both sheep and horse men, who were notorious for the small amount of land they owned or controlled by lease in proportion to their grazing operations, threw their influence against the movement. Sheepmen who had always drifted their flocks wherever they pleased now found themselves cut off from much desirable grazing land and water. The horse business in Texas had reached large proportions and fencing threatened its very existence. Indeed, large-scale range-horse operations have never been conducted successfully in a locality after fencing was universally adopted. Not only did fences serve as a barrier between water and their distant grazing lands, but many animals were also permanently and fatally injured by being cut into shreds by the barbed wire.

Thus, the small cowmen and the sheepmen and the horse men united against the large cow outfits. With the financial backing of those who ran sheep and horses, the three made a powerful combination. Neither did the cow outfits sit down and see their property destroyed and their plans disrupted without fighting back. They armed their regular men and hired others who were known for their quick trigger fingers. Before long the country consisted of two armed camps, with disinterested and neutral persons caught in between. On one side were the large cow outfits who were fast coming into public disfavor, and on the other was that group of unknown parties who rode at night and did their destructive work under cover of darkness. Those who felt that the cow outfits were within their legal rights, and that eventually all matters would adjust themselves, dared not say so. It was learned that the fence cutters could employ other means of hitting back besides cutting fences.

As far as the records go, there were never any pitched battles joined at night along the fence lines, but it is a miracle that there were not. Both factions had an array of armed men in the field, but, luckily, they never seemed to get together. The fence cutters had an adequate spying system, and they managed to conduct their operations at points that were unguarded. There were times when they burned off large tracts of grass and then set fire to buildings while the occupants were out fighting the prairie fire or guarding the fence lines.

Both factions adopted a tight-mouthed policy, and it was never common knowledge just what did take place. Actions of the cow outfits were exposed more or less to public view, but those of the fence cutters were clothed in secrecy. A few isolated and unmarked graves might have been connected up with missing men, but even their families refused to divulge their fate. There were times when an absentee's small holdings were disposed of and his family moved away to distant parts without anyone's knowing the reason why. It was never known whether he had lost his life in the conflict or whether he had found things too hot and skipped the country while skipping was good.

The cow outfits were at the disadvantage of always being on the defensive without knowing where the opposition would strike the next time. Local officers who earnestly tried to stop the disturbance worked under an effective handicap. It was easy enough to point the finger of suspicion at certain individuals, but proof was sadly lacking. Members of the outlaw bands refused to talk and others dared not to do so. Eventually, the local officers admitted their inability to handle the situation and called upon the governor for help. The chief executive assigned the Texas Rangers to the job of clearing up the trouble, and that body of fighting men went at the task as efficiently as they had fought the Indians in former days and broken up gangs of raiders along the Mexican border.

It was now discovered that there was no suitable law to prosecute the guilty parties in case of identification and arrest. Fencing was a new thing, and no one had thought of passing a law to prohibit destruction of fences. The penalty for malicious mischief was not considered to be severe enough punishment for one convicted for such an act. By the time the next session of the legislature convened, the cattlemen had the law ready for passage. It carried a heavy prison sentence for anyone convicted of the crime.

During this period of watchful waiting the Rangers were not idle. They had been working quietly for many months, gathering evidence in every county that was afflicted with the trouble. Upon a given date they acted in unison, and soon the jails were full of suspected fence cutters. In one instance, they locked up some of the county officials who were aiding and abetting the outlaw movement. Very few convictions were secured, however, because it was found out that most of the devilment had been done before passage of the new statute. While the entire affair ended in what might be termed a huge joke, results were obtained just as well. Many law-abiding men who had been drawn into the affair without due thought and had seen the error of their ways were glad to seize upon that opportunity to quit. It was a happy ending to what might have been the bloodiest conflict in the history of the state.

The small cowmen who elected to remain in the country reconciled themselves to the changing conditions and found equal opportunity with all. Sheepmen found it expedient to secure land for their grazing flocks. Unregenerate free rangers, and most horse men, either went out of business or drifted on to other states and territories where open free range was guaranteed by federal laws. With the problem of fencing settled for all time to come, cowmen proceeded to breed up their herds in a manner to their own choosing. Within twenty years, most traces of the Longhorns had been replaced by a sturdier, faster-growing, and more sightly animal.

For many years after the dawn of cattle history, little was known about the northern half of Texas. The only times the area had been penetrated by white men were while they were in pursuit of marauding Indians. Experience had taught white men the danger of extending their chases too far. They had learned that it was best for their own welfare to turn back when approaching a line running roughly from where the Rio Grande entered the state, near the present site of El Paso on the west, to the mouth of Pease River on the east. North of this line was no-man's land, which constituted the main stronghold of warring Indian tribes.

It was from here that the devastating and bloody raids were made upon the settlements to the south. It was to this region that the mounted hordes retreated when pursued by the Rangers or by army cavalry. There was little water in the area compared to the wide expanse of land it embraced. Much of the water was tainted with brackish alkali salts and was undrinkable. The good watering places were few and far between, and known only to the Indians. Above the Cap Rock, on top of the High Plains, was a seemingly limitless prairie of level land absolutely devoid of water except for the few rivers that cut their way across it, or the temporary lakes that formed during a rainy season.

The expanding cattle business encircled this area before it was ever invaded. Floyd Thompson had made his memorable drive through Kansas and had established the Abilene market. Goodnight and Loving had pushed their way across the waterless divide of West Texas, and up the Pecos through Raton Pass into

Colorado, where their herds spread over the Arkansas and South Platte valleys. John Chisum had established himself at the mouth of the Rio Hondo in New Mexico before a head of cattle was ever driven onto the Staked Plains by a white man. The Chisholm Trail to Abilene, and the trail to Dodge City, passed eastward into the Indian Territory of Oklahoma, while the Goodnight and Loving Trail swung westward and thence up the Pecos into Colorado. The Goodnight herds met other Texas cattle which had moved over the Dodge City Trail and up the Arkansas to Colorado, thus forming a complete circle around the unknown land.

An area consisting of more than a million square miles of virgin grassland was completely surrounded by grazing herds before the ranges of the Staked Plains were ever touched. This was partly due to the hostility of the Indians, lurking in the breaks along the Cap Rock, and dominating the High Plains, but the lack of sufficient water to sustain large herds of cattle was the principal reason that the region remained unclaimed.

Strange to say, the stocking of this area was started by a movement of cattle from the north instead of from the south. The flow of cattle has always been — and is even to this day — from south to north, but in this case the custom was reversed. It is also noteworthy that this movement was carried out by Charles Goodnight, who led the way in so many other phases of the cattle business. When he moved down from southern Colorado to the Palo Duro Canyon and established headquarters in the wild breaks of the upper Red River, he became the first cowman to venture into the shunned area.

When Goodnight approached the country, there were only two settlements in that broad expanse of prairie. Both of these were situated close to the northern edge along the Canadian River. One was named Tascosa, near the Texas-New Mexico border, and the other was Mobeetie, two hundred miles lower down upon the same stream. These were not cowtowns by any means. They were populated by trappers and buffalo hunters nearly as wild as the animals they stalked. These men were engaged primarily in slaughtering buffalos for their hides and the few cattle that any of them might have owned were merely incidental to their main vocation.

From his many scouting expeditions against Indians during the war, Goodnight had gained almost as thorough a knowledge of the country as had the Indians themselves. When he was ready to make his location, he knew exactly where to go. He spread his herds through the immense reaches of the Palo Duro, which was amply watered by the springs and head draws of one prong of the Red River. He found many buffalo grazing upon the flats of the Palo Duro, which he and his cowboys drove away in the van of his herd. He was also compelled to protect both his horses and cattle from the roving bands of Comanches who still passed back and forth through the canyons.

There were other streams bisecting this wide area, such as the Canadian, both forks of the Red, the Pease and the headwaters of the Brazos. In time, all the water in these streams came within the cowman's scope. The rivers were so few and far between that the amount of grazing land within the limit of a cow's travel between water and grass was infinitesimal compared to the wide expanses that lay outside the orbit. Grass grew in greatest abundance for miles upon miles, but there was no permanent water to make it usable. Thus, the matter rested this way until an instrument for probing deep into the earth to tap subterranean supplies of water had been invented and moved from Europe to the Eastern seaboard, and thence halfway across the continent to the cattle ranges.

Early in the nineteenth century in France, a means was being sought to secure drinking water from underground for city inhabitants, instead of from the polluted surface streams. A mechanic in the town of Artois succeeded in perfecting a machine capable of boring to great depths beneath the earth's surface. Unknowingly, this man made a valuable contribution to the advancement of the cattle industry. The fruits of his labors brought millions and millions of acres of arid grazing land into the cowman's sphere of operation.

It required many years for the deep-well boring machine to arrive in America. Many more years had to pass before it reached the dry land of the cattle range. The first ones to be employed in the western part of the country were operated by the United States Government in 1860. The purpose was not to locate underground water, but experiments were conducted to determine the mineral content of the earth's lower strata. Like many other projects and undertakings, the drillings were stopped by the outbreak of the War Between the States. When the need for underground water became manifest, the knowledge gained from those experimental drillings was put to use.

During the decade following the war, the era of gigantic railroad construction projects got under way. In some Western sections the rail lines which eventually spanned the continent stretched for miles upon miles without traversing a stream of living water fit for boiler use. Thus, it was the transcontinental railroads which first seized upon, and utilized, the deep-well machine for securing water of the proper elements and in necessary quantities. By perusing the logs left by the government drillers many years before, it was learned that an adequate supply of pure water could be tapped at varying depths, depending upon the locality.

Getting water to the top of the ground from a deep well offered little or no problem for the railroad companies. Pumps had been perfected long ago, and the railroads needed water in such large quantities they could afford the installation of steam pumping plants and the necessary personnel to man them. They had means of transporting and distributing fuel to the scattered stations at little or no cost. To an individual, such an arrangement was impossible.

The Western cowmen were keenly interested in this progressive development. They had watched prolific crops of grass, covering millions of acres, go to waste year after year, all for want of the necessary water to maintain their grazing herds. They longed to take advantage of the facilities employed by the rail lines, but they realized that such was beyond their financial reach. The first cost of boring the well was almost prohibitive, but that was a small item compared to the expense of the installation and operation of a pumping plant. The distance of a cow's travel back and forth between water and grass is limited to a few miles. It would have required many wells and pumps to water a tract of land large enough to carry a few thousand cattle. Cowmen needed many small power plants to be scattered widely over the range before they could take advantage of the benefits offered by the deep-well machine, and secure enough water to stock the arid lands. If they thought of the windmill at all, the idea was dismissed for the same reason of prohibitive cost.

Windmills have been in use just about as long as any other machinery in the world today. Their origin dates back many centuries in Europe. Designed for operating huge pumps, their purpose was to dispose of water instead of producing it for use. They were erected along dikes in the low coast countries, and pumped seepage water back into the sea. Slow and clumsy in operation, but hugely powerful, they had immense capacities for throwing water. There was no self-regulating device of automatic control for the giant wheels, and when the wind reached a certain velocity, it was necessary to shut the machines off altogether. For this reason, there had to be someone in attendance at all times.

It was conceivable that a smaller machine could be constructed for use in the cattle country along the same general principles embraced in the larger one. It would not have been feasible to keep a man on hand to manipulate the shut-off attachments every time a strong wind came up. High winds in the Plains country are constantly frequent, and such an arrangement would have required an attendant at every well and pumping plant. For this reason, it was to be many years after Charles

Goodnight moved into the Palo Duro before the Great Plains area could be fully stocked.

Like barbed wire, the windmill was introduced into the cattle country from another section. It was almost perfect in construction and operation when it arrived. In most districts east of the Mississippi, streams are close together with an abundant supply of water for all purposes. It was the universal custom for each farmhouse to have a well for family use, but these wells were relatively shallow, and were dug by hand with pick and shovel. Water was drawn to the surface in buckets by rope and pulley. In later years, pipe and hand pump were installed for use by the more progressive families.

But there were other localities in the humid farming land west of the Mississippi, where good surface water was not available the year round. Farmers were constantly pushing north and westward and settling upon the higher prairie land, where many of the streams did not contain permanent water. Thus, most people were compelled to rely more and more upon wells for both domestic and general use. In the higher country, the wells were necessarily of greater depth, and drawing water by means of buckets or hand pumps became quite a task for watering stock. This increased volume of labor set men to seeking an easier and quicker means of supplying themselves and their livestock with the needed water.

As stated before, some men had already availed themselves of the hand pump. Operation of the valves and cylinders was still a mystery to most people. As pumps came into more general use, there was opened up a field of service for so-called pump experts to keep them in repair. Such artisans were commonly known as pump doctors, and one of them was located in the village of Beloit, Wisconsin. While carrying on his trade, this man devoted much of his time and thought to the idea of a power lift for water by employing a windmill. He aroused the interest of a local blacksmith by the name of Holladay, who was said to have "a ready hand and quick turn of mind for making useful tools and instruments." Between the two of them, a working windmill was constructed and put into operation.

While this mill did draw water from one of the deepest wells in the neighborhood, it was far from being perfect. It could hardly have been called practical. Its chief defect was that age-old problem of self-regulating and governing. The first model was left unattended for a short time, and it beat itself to pieces during an unexpected, high windstorm. But the inventors had caught the idea, and they felt that they were on the road to success. After enlisting the financial backing of a farmer and capitalist in the community, they devoted their entire time to work and experiments. Eventually they succeeded, and they were able to create a mill that would slow down its revolutions with increasing velocity of wind, and would automatically shut itself off entirely during a storm. The first practical models were put on the market in 1867. It was years later before they reached the cattle country in abundance.

From that time on, the development and perfection of the windmill is a matter of history. Like the barbed wire, it did not reach full-scale production and sale without first running an expensive course in litigation. It is sufficient to say that, by the late Seventies, all legal contests were settled, and the manufacture of windmills and parts was fairly well standardized. As the continental railroads were the first to avail themselves of the deep-well drill, they were also the first to bring the windmill into general use in the Western country. Within twenty years after perfection, the stately tower and revolving wheel of the windmill marked the rail lines at intervals of every twenty miles or so. The steam pumping plants lay cold and idle, held in reserve to be used only in case of emergency, while the windmills did the work. It was not long after that until the Western cattlemen seized upon the windmill and adopted it for their own use.

After Charles Goodnight reached the Palo Duro with his herd and established himself, others followed his lead. They settled upon other streams in the country, and within a few years all land accessible to permanent surface water was stocked with grazing cattle. Even so, this constituted only a small part of the available range. There was still vastly more land lying idle for the lack of water than had been put to use in that vast territroy. After introduction of the deep well and windmill, all of the hitherto unused land was claimed for grazing.

Perfection and adoption of the windmill into general use was the means by which the remaining western half of the continent was brought into the cowman's sphere. While the windmill was used extensively all over the Great Plains area, by far the heaviest demand came from the unwatered lands of Texas. Nowhere in the northern half of this hemisphere were there greater areas with an abundance of grass without a natural stream. There were tracts embracing millions of acres without a drop of permanent water upon them. Large cow outfits covering five hundred or more square sections of land, and running twenty-five to fifty thousand cattle, came to rely entirely upon wells and windmills for their water supply.

Eventually wells came to be located at intervals of every few miles. Upon some ranches of the Plains country, it was said that a cow would never get more than two miles away from water. There was a time when a man riding across the plains would always be within sight of at least two windmills and sometimes a half dozen. Surplus water was stored in upground dirt tanks, which were enclosed in a fenced lot with the windmill. The water for consumption by the animals was piped underground outside and flowed by gravity to a string of troughs. The flow was controlled by float valves. As the adoption of hand pumps in the eastern prairie land had opened up a new line of work, so did the use of windmills upon the large ranches of the West. One or more men were assigned to the exclusive job of oiling and keeping mills and pumps in working condition.

It can be said that invention of the deep-well machine and the windmill threw more land open for grazing than any other event in world history. Stocking of the entire Great Plains area was now complete. From the Missouri to the Pacific Coast; from the Rio Grande to the Canadian Steppes, cattle ranged over every acre of land that was capable of growing grass. It would be safe to say that this combination made grazing land available for ten million more head of cattle.

CHAPTER NINE
COW THIEVES
AND RANGE WARS

I T WAS a long and uphill struggle for cowmen to bring their industry to a point of stabilization. The trade has always been, and still is, to a certain extent, a financial gamble, but at one time those who engaged in the calling gambled with their lives as well as with their fortunes. At first it was the Indians who preyed upon them with ruthless ferocity. In later years, bands of organized thieves operated openly and brazenly wherever livestock were handled in large numbers. Sheepherders and horse men were eternally encroaching upon what cowmen considered to be their domain by right of conquest. The most annoying, and what proved to be the eventual destructive agency, was the homesteaders who persistently spread themselves over the Western prairies.

It has always been so that any undertaking which involved large sums of money attracted certain classes who figured to live off the earning of other people. In the cattle business, thieves found a perfect setup for their operations. Although punishment was violent and certain if the thief was caught in the act, the chances of detection were slight, and the stakes were high. Cattle grazed over vast areas of unfenced land, and it was impossible for the owner to keep a close watch over them. Early-day cowmen kept poor records, or none at all, and it was seldom that a large operator could tell within a thousand head of how many he owned. Fifty or a hundred taken from one range, and a like amount from another, might never be missed at all, but certainly the shortage would not be discovered before the next spring roundup, when a reasonably accurate count might be secured. Thus, a bunch of stolen animals could reach a huge total and be disposed of before the theft was discovered.

At one time there was no law to protect a man's stock except what he and his own men could effect. A wise man never embarked upon a new venture without sufficient men and arms to give him at least a fighting chance. John Chisum knew this when he made his location in the wilds of New Mexico. Charles Goodnight knew it when he drove the remnant of his herds down into the forbidden area of the Panhandle and located in the Palo Duro Canyon.

Naturally, measures taken by cowmen to protect their property against depredations of others frequently ended in violent conflict. The longest and bloodiest of these eruptions was the Lincoln County War in New Mexico, but it was not the only one by any means. Outbreaks flared at many different points over the range land, and they continued up to the latter part of the nineteenth century. The Lincoln County War raged through the late Seventies and early Eighties, but the Johnson County War in Wyoming did not take place until in the Nineties. The Tanto Basin War in Arizona was fought out during the Eighties, while in-between periods were spotted with lesser conflicts, which were not deemed of sufficient importance to receive general notice and be recorded.

Outside of private feuds between families and clans, and the fence wars, Texas was generally free from disputes of this kind which led to violence. As explained in a previous chapter, the state vested individuals or companies with the right to acquire tracts of land either by outright purchase or long-term leases. This gave Texas cowmen a firmer grasp upon the range where their cattle grazed, and there was little or no trouble over range or water rights. It was the days of Reconstruction that produced the most violence between men of the same race in the state's history.

As the evils of that unhappy era spread into all walks of life and every undertaking, they also had their effect upon the cattle business. Carpetbag politicians, who held all public offices, set up official decrees for regulation of the cattle trade. They appointed brand inspectors, who collected illegal and exorbitant fees for inspecting herds moving out of the state. It became a common thing for inspectors to connive with thieves and accept forged bills of sale as genuine documents and permit them to drive large numbers of stolen cattle from the country. In the sparsely settled areas the state police, which was the only law-enforcement agency, could, or would, do little to preserve peace.

Out on the frontier where cattle were grazed, violence seemed to rage the fiercest. Besides the hostility that existed between the citizens and the officeholders, other elements entered into affairs which fanned the flames of hatred. Union sympathizers, who had found things too hot for them to remain in the country during the war, now returned, seeking revenge. They brought along with them friends and relatives who were ready to fatten themselves at the expense of a prostrate people. The Texans also had a score of their own to settle. They could remember how certain individuals had grabbed everything they could carry away with them when the country was without protection of able-bodied men. Thus, the different factions went for each other with blood in their eyes.

It came to a point where one man was afraid to trust his nearest neighbor, and no one dared voice an open opinion upon issues of the day. Armed mobs rode at night, leaving a trail of death and destruction in their wake. Few men dared to be caught out after dark or to turn a light on in their house. Men had been called to their front doors and shot down, with their lamps forming a background. Others had been taken forcibly from their homes and hanged without apparent cause or reason. All through the period of Reconstruction the conflict raged, becoming worse day by day. After civil rights were restored to the population and they were allowed to elect their own public officials, law and order gradually returned. With the Indian menace coming under control and with the yoke of Reconstruction thrown from its neck, the cattle business was ready to move ahead to its glorious development.

Outside of Reconstruction losses and the gigantic losses from Indian raids, which will be told in more detail later on, Texas was fairly free from depredations of organized bands of cattle thieves. Here again, the privilege of absolute range control operated to the advantage of the Texas cowman. He had little or no homestead problem to contend with, and after fencing became general, it was still more difficult for thieves to operate in and out of pastures. Theft of cattle in Texas was confined generally to unscrupulous trail drivers who gathered other cattle along the way and absorbed them into their own herds. Local cattlemen soon remedied this situation when they organized themselves into an association and located competent brand men at strategic points along the trail, with legal authority to stop all trail herds and cut from them all brands belonging to the membership.

It was in other states, which came under the jurisdiction of the Federal land laws, and where free grazing was open to all alike, that wholesale thefts occurred and disputes between the farmers and cow outfits flared into violence. Cattle in the open-range countries spread over wide areas during summer months, and they drifted great distances during the winter, with no fence or other obstruction to hold them in restraint. It was not uncommon to see brands of an outfit fifty or seventy-five miles away from the home range. There were few riders abroad during the off season, and it was little or no trick at all for a gang of slick cow thieves to ply their trade. By driving at night and hiding out in the daytime, a sizable bunch of cattle could be driven a long distance with only a slight chance of detection.

Policy of the Federal Government in land affairs was detrimental to the open-range cowman's interests. Glowing inducements were put out for homesteaders to settle upon the Western plains, and these brought a flock of settlers to the territory. As a matter of course, the settlers located their homesites upon living water, which fact interfered more or less with the free coming and going of range stock. There were many times when a homesteader awoke to find his fences down and his crops trampled by herds of range cattle. They had to even the score in some way, and many of them sought to adjust matters by slaughtering a fat beef now and then. Such matters did not serve to improve relationship between the homesteaders and the cattle owners. It was inevitable that the man with the plow and the man on horseback should come into conflict sooner or later just as they had around Abilene, Ellsworth and Dodge City years before.

During this time a change was coming over the cattle business. In the open range states where little or no land

ownership was required for grazing great herds of cattle, corporations were being formed. Capitalists in the East and as far
away as Europe were being attracted by the prospects of easy
money in cattle and ranching. The newly formed combinations
absorbed the scant land holdings and stock of many individuals and spread their controls over wide areas. No one, and
especially not the homesteaders, held any special regard for
these unknown owners of the huge cow outfits who purport-
edly lived in style and comfort in remote places and who were
coldly indifferent to the plight of the men who were trying to
make a poor living from the ground. Not even the cowboys
who were paid to take care of the property of the non-resident
owners felt the same loyalty toward them that had bound
them to such operators as Goodnight, Chisum, Loving and
Blocker, who lived with their men and shared all hardships
and dangers with them.

Far from expectations, the homesteaders found life hard and
cruel upon the bleak prairies. Crop failures and nonexistent markets for the pitiful products they did raise drove many of them to
despondency and desperation. It is no wonder that many of them
fell before temptation and butchered a beef now and then from
among the thousands that surrounded their forlorn homesteads.
It is no wonder that many of them became ready and willing at
times to aid and abet a professional cow thief when an opportunity offered itself.

Employees of the cattle companies who were on the ground
realized the desperate and uphill fight the homesteaders were
making to keep themselves and families alive. With the traditional spirit of generosity inherent in all cowboys of that day
and time, they were inclined to overlook the occasional theft of
a single animal. One thing led to another, however, and the first
thing anyone knew, some of those starving homesteaders turned
out to make first-class cattle thieves. Instead of being satisfied
with enough beef to keep themselves, they started selling it in

the markets of the distant towns and settlements. Some joined forces with professional thieves, while others struck out boldly on a course of their own and began to moonshine bunches of cattle out of the country.

Like the first settlers in Texas, the early homesteaders of the West were not cowmen by any means. They knew little or nothing about handling range stock, and most of them were poor horsemen. In a sparsely settled area, where places were far apart and horses were plentiful, no man ever remained afoot very long. Those homesteaders of the Western plains secured horses, and they learned to ride and rope and brand cattle just as the Texans had done for fifty years before.

Some learned all the tricks there were to know about stealing cattle. They found out that the only way to prove ownership of an unbranded calf was the brand its mother carried, and they learned to work ahead of the spring or branding roundup and throw unbranded calves and their mothers around behind the drives, and then wait patiently for the calves to be weaned. It was then safe to claim and brand them as their own and add them to their small holdings of cattle. They learned to run a bonafide brand into a bogus one with such skill that it took the closest scrutiny of an expert brand man to detect the fraud. They learned to ride at night and drive stolen cattle from the country by moonlight with a measure of safety.

Depredations against Western stockmen continued with mounting volume. So acute was feeling against the large cow outfits that most of the homesteaders who were not actually engaged in thefts openly sympathized with the thieves. As a measure to protect themselves against this costly nuisance, associations of cattlemen were formed over different parts of the country. They hired undercover men to work as stock detectives and secure evidence against the suspects. Instead of furnishing the evidence to regularly constituted authorities for prosecution, at least one association in central and eastern Wyoming embarked on a program that was far more illegal and cowardly than were the deeds of the most notorious cattle thieves.

This particular association styled themselves as the Regulators, and they attempted the rawest deal that was ever perpetrated in a civilized country. Their first act was to hire professional killers to rid themselves of known thieves and a few obnoxious homesteaders by shooting them from ambush. A great many men met death from these hired assassins' bullets. The climax to this cold-blooded undertaking came when the notorious Tom Home was arrested and convicted and hanged at Cheyenne for the murder of a homesteader's fifteen-year-old son whom he mistook for the father. It has been said that many rich cattlemen and officials of the association were literally shaking in their boots for fear the killer would divulge the names of his employers before he was executed. However, he remained true to his creed and met his doom with sealed lips which carried the secret to his grave.

The individual killings did not stop the theft of cattle, and the Regulators adopted a more drastic and bloodthirsty policy. If it had not been for a single incident, no doubt this undertaking would have resulted in the most violent and destructive episode in range cattle history. It is difficult to believe that men who were owners of property and who regarded themselves as law abiding citizens would institute and sanction such an illegal movement against people of an area larger than some states, and as late as the last decade of the last century. The country at that time was under the jurisdiction of local government agencies, but the cattlemen chose to take measures into their own hands and punish the offenders with their own methods.

At Cheyenne, a mixed train bound for an unknown destination was set in motion. It carried fifty hard-faced gunmen with horses, wagons, camp equipment, ammunition and enough provisions to sustain such a force for an indefinite time. The outfit detrained at a blind siding in northern Wyoming and, still clothed in secrecy, the force moved stealthily forward. Its objective was to eradicate all cattle thieves and their sympathizers, which would have taken in most of the population of the country.

They approached the buildings of a ranch which was said to be the hangout of notorious cattle thieves. It is not known how many they expected to find in the hiding place, but subsequent events developed that there were only two. Under cover of darkness the place was surrounded, and the possemen waited impatiently for the break of day. Then without warning of any kind and without their victims being given a chance to surrender, one of them was shot down and fatally wounded when he emerged from the house with water bucket in his hand and started toward a well a short distance away. When his startled companion heard the shots and came to the door, he was met with a fusillade of bullets. In spite of lead spattering all around, he rescued his wounded companion and carried him into the shelter of the house. Then the battle started.

All day long that cornered cow thief stood off a force of fifty men, who were determined to get him. In the afternoon his partner died, leaving him all alone. Besides keeping his enemies at a safe distance and ministering to his dying companion, he managed to put in writing a narrative of the day's events. Fortunately this diary fell into neutral hands and was preserved. The ungrammatical record made by that desperate man while he fought for his life is one of the most unique documents ever written. The brief account of that day-long battle scrawled upon the leaves of a notebook draws a clearer picture of Western character and traditions than an ordinary writer could describe in a two thousand-word manuscript. It proved to be his final message to this mortal world.

At no time did he admit his guilt, but neither did he deny it. He seemed to know exactly what the others intended to do to him, but no expression of remorse or self-pity ever crept into the record. He never wrote a single derogatory word against those who were after his life. In one passage he made the simple state-ment: "It don't look like they aim to let me get away this time."

He never knew for certain who they were, but it appears that he made a fairly close guess. He said in his writings that one looked like —— and another like ——, but the names were thoroughly blotted out before the notebook was surrendered for public inspection. He never mentioned receiving a call to sur-render, and he never indicated that he would have accepted one if it had come. He seemed to know that it was a fight to death and that his chances of escape were very slight indeed.

The Regulators learned that no particular person had a cor-ner on personal bravery. Their victim displayed more courage during the one-sided battle than any of them showed that day. He braved their fire long enough to rescue his wounded com-rade, while none of them dared to come within range of his guns and expose themselves to his fire. For individual coolness under hopeless circumstances, the actions of that outlaw have never been surpassed. Had he been aligned upon the side of law and order, his exploits would have been widely publicized, and his name would have been enshrined upon the honor roll of history along with other heroes.

All day long, he stood off a force of fifty heavily armed men from that lonely cabin upon the Wyoming plains. The climax came soon after nightfall. Moving again under the cover of dark-ness, the possemen set fire to a wagonload of hay. They let the wagon roll downhill under its own momentum and crash into one side of the house. This ignited the building, and the besieged cow thief was forced to come out from his hiding place, or be burned to death.

Before attempting to run the gauntlet of fifty gunmen hover-ing all around the burning house — but safely outside its orbit of light — he took time to record the fact that the house had been set on fire and he would have to leave. He said goodbye to every-body, "if I never see you again," and then signed his full name.

He was shot down and instantly killed by a score or more of bullets — one of which passed through the notebook in his breast shirt pocket. If he killed any of his assailants, they were buried without public knowledge.

In the meantime, the operation had been discovered. A neighbor of the condemned man, while riding over the range, was attracted by the shooting. He approached the place with caution, but he was sighted. The possemen made a futile attempt either to kill or capture the prying homesteader, but he made his escape. Riding as desperately as Paul Revere had done more than a hundred years before, he spread the news. The homesteaders answered his call and rallied from far and near. Before the Regulators could make another move, they were met by a howling mob of outraged homesteaders with blood in their eyes.

The Regulators realized they were in a tight fix. They formed a line of battle behind the protection of a hill and waited for the charge they thought to be coming. Before being entirely surrounded, they managed to get a runner away to the nearest military post with a desperate appeal for help. They had shunned and dodged all legal authority or sanction when starting out on their mission, but now that conditions were reversed and it looked as if they were about to be exterminated, they called loudly upon the law to rescue them.

When the homesteaders saw they had their enemies surrounded and at their mercy, they decided to starve them out. For four days they laid siege to the helpless posse, which had started out so confidently a short time before. This line of tactics turned out fortunately for the Regulators. They had been cut off from their supply base at the railroad and were entirely out of food and almost out of ammunition. The army intervened in the nick of time to save them. Within another day or so, there would have been a bloody battle fought upon the Wyoming prairies. It would have resulted in the death of many homesteaders and perhaps of all the possemen.

With the army furnishing a protective escort, the crew of expert gunmen and self-styled Regulators slunk back to their place of starting. They boarded their special train and were dispersed upon arrival at Cheyenne. The above disturbance resulted in the known death of only two men, but the provident intervention of the army kept it from becoming the bloodiest epoch in cattle history.

Besides their struggle against Indians, homesteaders and thieves, cowmen were faced with another vexatious problem when sheep invaded the rangeland. It has been proven lately that, under proper management, both cattle and sheep will thrive upon the same range, but it was not so at one time. Sheep went altogether under their herder's guidance, but cattle ran loose and went where they pleased. There was something about the odor left by sheep wherever they grazed that cattle did not like. Thus, when flocks of sheep drifted into a certain range, most of the cattle took off for other parts. As both types of animals spread over the ranges, they were bound to meet at more places than one. Violence resulted many times in different localities, but the sheepmen came out winners in most contests.

Again, Texas was practically free from this strife. When a cowman or sheepman secured control of a certain block of land, there were no grounds for contention by the other. Such was not the case in other range states, where the law gave each individual equal right to graze the public domain.

The most noteworthy and bloody eruptions between sheep and cattlemen took place in the Tanto Basin of Arizona. It is fairly illustrative of the many disturbances that occurred at various intervals and places over the country. A group of cattlemen headed by the Graham family held control over the Tanto Basin. Large sheep interests of California decided to invade the area with their flocks. They engaged a clan of caretakers and herders, consisting of old man Tewksberry and his half-breed Indian sons and daughters, with their families. There were several thousand sheep in the movement, with indications of more to come. The cattlemen served their customary notice for the care-takers to keep their charges outside certain bounds. The notice was ignored, and soon the bleating sheep were spreading over the choice ranges of the Tanto.

From accounts of those in close touch with the situation, it appears that the cowmen were reluctant to take a drastic step. It is not known whether they sensed a premonition of what was to come, or whether they sincerely desired to avoid bloodshed. It is not a matter of record who fired the first shot in the fray, but it is well known who fired the last one. The feud raged for year after year, and before it ended, men became involved who were not even remotely connected with the issues when it started. Even sons of the principals grew up to sacrifice their lives before it was over. The heritage of those half-breed Indians seemed to give them a decided advantage in the conflict. They proved to be craftier stalkers and more adept at setting ambush traps than were the impetuous cowmen. In the end, all of the Graham fam-ily and most of their supporters were dead, while most of the Tewksberry clan were still alive.

Organized bands of American cow thieves took a heavy toll of stock all over the range country. The spoils from their cunning operations amounted to a tremendous sum, but even so, all of it added together would look like a penny ante game compared to exploits of the Indian thieves and Mexican traders. This combi-nation perfected the grandest and most far reaching organization of cattle thieves ever known to the world. Neither was it with-out color, as will be shown later in this account. Depredations against ranches started before the outbreak of the War Between the States and lasted for years afterward.

This illicit trade, which reached huge proportions, was dominated by Spaniards and Mexicans from around Santa Fe and Las Vegas, New Mexico. It was they who supplied the appro-priate names given to people and places where the transactions occurred. Indeed, those engaged in the traffic were known as *Comancheros,* which was the general Spanish term for anyone who dealt with the Comanche Indians. It involved thousands of personnel, including every tribe of horse-riding, and fighting Indians that roamed the Great Plains area.

Ever since the first attempts to settle the Southwest, and the introduction of horses, Indians were the most persistent horse thieves ever known. They seemed to have acquired the trait by natural heritage, along with their expertness at ambush fighting. It has been noted how the early Spanish settlers complained that the Indians had rather steal gentle horses than to catch and tame the wild ones. In later years, they retained their instincts of accomplished horse thieves, and added the art of cattle stealing to their long string of other vices.

As long as buffalo were plentiful, the Indians paid little or no attention to cattle. In time they found that cattle not only made a satisfactory food substitute to replace the vanishing buffalo but they learned that these animals were also a medium of exchange for valuable goods which they needed. Thus, the Indians evolved into the greatest and most effective cow thieves of all times. They stole thousands and thousands of both cattle and horses in their many raids and got away with them in such a clever manner that it would put any white American thief to shame. For years they were able to elude the sharp eyes of the wisest frontiersmen. They perfected a means of scattering stolen animals in such a thorough manner that they left no trail to follow. They drove them to their hideouts in the badlands at the foot of the Staked Plains and disposed of them in a unique and crafty manner.

In that vast spread of land known as the Llano Estacado, and in the rough breaks at the foot of the Cap Rock, lurked the hostile Indian tribes of the Southwest. No American citizen knew anything about the mysteries of the region. Later events proved that to the Spanish traders from the headwaters of the Rio Grande and the Pecos, the country was an open book. Long before any law-abiding white men ventured into the depths and lived to return and tell about it, there were well-defined roads leading from one watering place to another, from the southeastern breaks of the escarpment into northern New Mexico. There were deep ruts cut into the grassy turf by Mexican *carreta* wheels and worn trails made by the hooves of the large herds of cattle and horses that had been driven across the land.

It was in the secluded brakes under the southern edge of the Cap Rock that the Mexican traders with their finished goods, and the Indian thieves with their stolen livestock, met on common ground and made their exchange. On this occasion they met on equal terms for mutual good, and a temporary truce was declared and respected. The Mexicans were certain of a safe return journey with the newly acquired livestock back to their own settlements four hundred miles away. The traders brought useful things, and the Indians wanted them to come again. Elsewhere, and in normal times, the Indians preyed upon Mexicans the same as whites. Neither would one of the traders have hesitated to slit an Indian's throat for a buffalo robe at any other time or place.

It is certain that the Indians got the worst of the bargains. Their consolation was that the commodity they had to trade cost them nothing more than the risk they ran while stealing it, and the things they got in exchange could be had in no other way. Whisky was one of the most popular items the *Comancheros* had to offer. After the Indians adopted the white man's weapon, powder and lead, and bullet molds, and eventually repeating rifles with cartridge ammunition ranked high upon the preferred list of goods.

From Mexican gulf ports had come these articles over the long and tortuous inland route, by two-wheeled *carretas,* through central Mexico and thence up the Rio Grande to headquarters at Santa Fe. After resale and distribution to various traders, they eventually reached their final destination at the southern foot of the Texas plains. Indeed, guns and ammunition that had been manufactured at Hartford, Bridgeport and Patterson found their way to the trading grounds. For many years, white men puzzled at the source of modern guns in possession of the Indians. It was not uncommon for a Texas Ranger or a United States Cavalryman to pick up from beside the body of an Indian slain in battle the latest model of American-made repeating rifle. After discovery of the *Comanchero* trail, the matter was no longer a mystery.

True to a Mexican's keen sense of observation and picturesque imagination, the meeting places were appropriately named. The largest and most popular was known as the *Río de las Lenguas,* or Tongue River. During a rendezvous, almost every tongue of the North American Continent was in spoken evidence. The various languages mingled with the dialect of the Comanche, Cheyenne, Apache, and Kiowa Indian tribes. Guttural mutterings of the Sioux, who had traveled from their stronghold in the Dakota Badlands to participate in the events, could be heard among the throngs. There were sharp accents of the French Canadians, and, to the shame of the American people, many of the conversations were carried on in English, spoken by men who had forsaken their own race and joined hands with the perpetual enemies.

It was to this place that the Indians brought stolen cattle and horses they had acquired from raids upon settlements along the Brazos, the Trinity, the Colorado, the Llanos and numerous other streams. It was here the stolen animals were bartered away for Mexican wares. While the Indians came more or less in large groups, the *Comancheros* came singly and in pairs and in companies. There were rich Dons, traveling in style and comfort in the finest carriages, and attended by a retinue of servants. They had peon slaves to drive their *carreta* trains of merchandise, and then to become herders for the stolen stock. There were groups of families, and the lone trader with a single *carreta,* or pack mule, with his meager lot of goods to be bargained for the greatest number of horses or cattle possible. Here in this great unexplored wilderness of Texas, where no human foot had ever trod except those engaged in the illicit trade, the two classes met on common ground, with the understanding that no violence would be committed.

While the trading ground of the *Río de las Lenguas* was the principal one, there was another spot where a select group carried out their business transactions. The Mexicans also supplied a fitting name for this place. It was called the *Valle de las Lágrimas* or The Valley of Tears, which immediately suggests sorrow. Only a few of the highest ranking Indian chiefs were admitted to this gathering. Negotiations were conducted by hard-faced white men, and cold-eyed *Comancheros,* with the few Indians as silent witnesses. No exchange of goods was made or even considered among this crowd. The commodity for sale was human beings, which traffic brought a given number of yellow gold coins counted across a blanket spread upon the ground.

The rich Spanish Dons, with their great *haciendas* of cultivated fields deep in the interior of Mexico, were eternally in need of slave labor. They were willing to pay good money for it, and the Comanches were delighted to supply their needs. This new side line was not only a good source of revenue, but it furnished also a wonderful opportunity to punish their peacefully inclined cousins, who had surrendered themselves to the white man's will.

The horse-riding, and fighting Indians of the Plains area had nothing but contempt for the less warlike tribes who had remained afoot, and had made peace with the white man. The arrogant Comanches hated these peaceful Indians more than they hated the white men, and respected them less. They had made war upon them at every opportunity, but after learning they were worth something alive, it was more satisfactory to capture and sell them into slavery than to kill them. The disgrace of being sold as a slave was considered worse than death. Thus, the eastern part of Texas was penetrated in daring raids, with slave material as the object. It was a sad day for those unfortunate beings when they fell prey to these raiding parties.

The question might well be raised as to why Spaniards from Mexico would go to all that trouble to secure slaves in the United States when there were plenty of subjects among the Indians of their own country. There is a good reason for it. It is true that their political influence would permit them to enslave some of their own Indians, but that practice had not proved satisfactory. Those impressed into servitude near home were always escaping and returning to their old hideouts in the mountain wilderness. On the other hand, timid and inoffensive captives brought from a distant land were more submissive. After being captured and maltreated by the cruel and vengeful members of their own race until time of delivery to their new masters, what little spirit they may have had would be entirely broken. The thousand-mile march in chains into Mexico confused and bewildered them until they were robbed of any incentive to escape.

None but the young and able-bodied were in demand. It was here in the Valle de las Lágrimas that the miserable captives were herded together like so much stock and bargained for the highest sums of money obtainable. Those who failed to meet approval of the purchasers were shunted to one side and slaughtered without mercy. Sisters and brothers, and fathers and mothers, were torn apart to satisfy the needs of various buyers. The prettiest maidens were kept separate for another kind of market. Eventually, they found sale among certain individuals who bought them for vicious desires of their own. They must have been sad events indeed, if the Mexican traders — who were entirely without sentiment — were moved to name this trading ground the Valley of Tears.

The Indian slaves sold for money counted across a spread saddle blanket were not the only type of human beings that figured in the transactions. Now and then a white child captured on some destructive raid was bartered and sold. Through a whim, and not from mercy, a Cheyenne brave once abducted two children after the war party had killed the parents during a raid upon a Kansas settlement. Jesse Chisholm, a half-breed Cherokee trader, discovered them and immediately bought them from their captor. He restored them to their nearest relatives, but never received nor asked for a cent of the purchase price.

Jesse Chisholm died in 1868, which event broke all contact between the hostile tribes and the white men. He had established a precedent, however, and the Indians reasoned correctly that if one white man would pay a ransom for a captured child, another would do it also. It took a long time for them to convince the hard-bargaining *Comancheros* that somewhere there was a white man who was willing to pay good money for the release of a captive white child. If the renegade traders who participated in the affairs of the Río de las Lenguas and the Valle de las Lágrimas brought shame to their race, others brought credit when they unselfishly paid out sums of money to ransom unknown captive children from the Indians. Thus, for years, the *Comanchero* trade flourished before any law abiding white man knew of its existence. For years, cowmen lost huge numbers of their stock through Indian raids without the least inkling as to their ultimate disposition. It was later estimated by competent authorities that more than a hundred thousand horses and three hundred thousand cattle followed the unknown trail. In due time these animals found their way to the trading grounds beneath the Cap Rock and thence across the high plains into northern Mexico.

For years, army cavalrymen and Texas Rangers puzzled at the source of modern, American-made firearms that the Indians used against them in battle. For years, substantial citizens of the country were approached by sly-eyed merchants from Monterrey and other Mexican towns with information about captive white children in custody of American Indians. There is no estimate of the number of Indian slaves and captive children that changed hands during these times.

Strange to say, the one who figured most prominently in pioneer cattle history was responsible for the discovery and exposure of the gigantic thieving operations. When Charles Goodnight and Oliver Loving were making one of their drives up the Pecos, thieves stole some of their saddle horses. Goodnight and the fighting cowboy known as One-Armed Bill Wilson followed the trail into the wild breaks east and south of Las Vegas. They did not succeed in capturing the thieves or locating their horses, but they found something much more interesting. In a secluded valley they ran onto a number of cows wearing Goodnight's *C V* brand. He recognized many of these animals as some of the herd he had lost during a raid the Indians made upon him in north central Texas three years before, and at a place six or seven hundred miles away.

Goodnight rode forthwith to Las Vegas, where he secured the services of a lawyer and filed a replevin action in court for recovery of the stolen cattle. He lost the suit because the Mexican judge had no sympathy or friendship for a Texas cattleman. Undaunted by his setback, he carried out an extensive investigation. His findings resulted in a daring recovery of many stolen cattle, belonging to himself and other victims of Indian raids.

At the risk of being shot from ambush by hostile residents, the two Texans prowled through the country around the small village of Puerta de las Lunas. They found that the comparatively small number of cattle involved in the lawsuit was only a fraction of those wearing old Texas brands scattered throughout the hills. The calves following the cows wore Spanish brands of local Mexican residents. Convinced that a gigantic system of cattle stealing was in operation, they continued with their investigation. They spent much time in the vicinity and questioned every Mexican they met. At length, Goodnight was able to piece together many strands of the mystifying puzzle. His widespread inquiries led to the discovery of the *Comanchero* trail.

He concluded that the organization was far too big for one man or a group of individuals to tackle. He had already learned the fallacy of making a fight through the local courts. He carried his information to the nearest military post and sought help from the army. He was told by the commanding officer that the army had no authority to act in such a matter. Failing in this, he embarked upon another and far more effective course.

He spread the news of his discovery over the cattle country of Texas. If Goodnight had hesitated at the thought of going after the proposition, either alone, or with another group of individuals, he found men who were not averse to taking matters in their own hands. A force of a hundred men who knew how to handle cattle and manipulate firearms was quickly assembled. They turned their horses toward New Mexico and rode up the Pecos Valley to the mountain foothills. They then swung around, wing fashion, and started back. They breasted through a strip of country fifty miles wide, and rounded up the eastern half of the territory. They held all animals wearing Texas brands, and before the drive was over, they drifted a loose mass of ten thousand cattle. It is fitting to say that men riding Goodnight horses participated in that vast roundup.

The trail of this monstrous herd was dogged by sheriffs and deputies and constables, bearing warrants of arrest and other legal papers which were never served. Even in that land of brave and reckless men, there was no one who dared go up against that array of determined cowmen. Eventually, the giant herd reached the Texas border and passed out of the New Mexico courts' jurisdiction. It was then split up into wieldy bunches and moved back to the rightful ranges.

While Goodnight was not successful in getting the army to take action against the *Comanchero* traders, the information he supplied was responsible for destruction of the ring. All Comanche Indians had been assigned to their reservation by the Government, in what is now the present state of Oklahoma.

When they departed from the confines, they were considered out of bounds, and subject to discipline. After Goodnight made his startling discovery, the army took action and caught the main body of the Comanche Tribe hiding in the breaks beneath the Cap Rock. A decisive battle was fought, which resulted in the slaughter of many braves and destruction of all their horses. Thus, left miles and miles from food and shelter, the remnants of the band plodded painfully to their reservation on foot. They suffered untold hardships during the trip, with many of the women and children dying from starvation and exposure.

It was the last time that the great tribe of Comanche Indians was able to assemble in force. For three hundred years they had carried on a bitter fight for supremacy in what they considered their own country. Slowly and relentlessly their enemies had been closing about them. It was indeed a sad event for a once proud and haughty race when, upon that fateful day, they made their last stand against the white men and superior arms. The battle and subsequent disastrous retreat was not only the blow that ended their career as a warring tribe, but it sounded the death knell to the *Comanchero* trade.

CHAPTER TEN
THE COW PONY

I T WOULD NOT be proper to attempt a saga of the cattle industry
without giving the cow pony his share in the story. In fact, it
can be correctly argued that he played the most important role
of all the other elements. Without him, the great industry which
spread over the western half of the continent within a few years
could never have been conducted successfully. The old time cow

pony arose to great heights of glory, and his breed was the foundation for a still better class of animals.

Horses have always played an important part in world history. No race of people who did not use them has ever amounted to anything. It was the lack of transportation which kept the Plains Indians in a degraded and pitiful state of existence. It was the horse that transformed them from impotent footmen to resourceful and dangerous warriors. Until the inclusion of mechanized armor in the armies, no country has ever won a war without a force of mounted soldiery. Even to this day, no general staff is willing to abandon cavalry altogether.

It has been shown in the initial chapter how the wild horses of America got their start. The animals left here by the invading Spaniards were of Arabian blood. This breed has always been noted for its superior qualities as cavalry horses, or any other class of saddle stock. Indeed, it was the foundation of our present-day race and saddle animals. In spite of springing from the same source, there is a vast difference between the horses in existence today and their wild cousins which roamed the Texas prairies during the early part of the last century.

It is a fact among animals as well as people that one branch of a family sometimes goes up while the other goes down. In this case, the wild mustang sank almost to the lowest depths. For three hundred years, the offspring of those Spanish cavalry horses ran free and unrestrained and undisturbed by man. During that period, inbreeding was rampant, and the once graceful cavalry horses degenerated into scrawny little animals with heavy manes and tales, and with nothing else striking in appearance about them. In another hundred years, the strain would have been beyond recovery.

The Mexican ranchers stopped the downhill plunge of deterioration when they instituted the art of selective breeding among the gentle stock. They found that a gelding was more tractable, more dependable, and more serviceable under all conditions than either a mare or a stallion. In time this knowledge was absorbed by the Indians. The practice of selective breeding stopped further deterioration and made for some improvement in the general character and class of the animals. Thus, by the time the first white settlers reached Texas, they found the Mexicans with a fair grade of horses and the Indians well supplied with riding stock which was considerably better than the thousands of animals that ran wild without restraint.

The first English-speaking people to settle in Texas were poor in worldly goods and there were few horses among them. It was seldom that one family owned more than one, and many families had none at all. Horses were employed altogether as a means of transportation, and oxen were the principal draft animals. When the rank and file went from one place to another, it was usually afoot. However, those pioneers did not remain afoot very long. In one way or another, each man soon came into ownership of riding stock, and it was found that a decided improvement resulted in a single cross-breeding of the wild mustang with gentler and better-blooded animals from the East. While it took several crosses for the offspring to acquire a respectable size, and to build and erase all traces of its wild ancestry, each cross made a creditable showing.

By the end of the war for Texas Independence, horses were fairly plentiful. Indeed, some men embarked in horse raising as a separate business and found it profitable to trap the wild mustangs and cross-breed them with other strains. A considerable number of the increase found a ready market among those who were venturing into cattle raising and whose growing herds caused an increasing need for additional horses to take care of the expanding business.

Like the cattle trade, the horse industry went through a period of broad expansion and prosperity. The range-horse business in America is entitled to a place in history, but it is mentioned here only insofar as it touches upon the cattle business. As a general rule, cow ponies were never exploited commercially. Like a carpenter's or a blacksmith's tools, they were considered as a necessary adjunct to the cattle trade. They were never broken and trained for the open market, and few of them were ever sold except under certain conditions. It would have been just about as easy to talk a cowman into giving up one arm or an eye as to trade him out of a first-class cutting horse. In general, the sale of cow ponies was merely incidental to another transaction — such as selling a ranch with all stock, or selling a herd of cattle with the saddle horses going in the bargain, or selling off unfit or surplus animals.

Descendants of the wild mustangs, which eventually came to be known as the Spanish pony, were not pretty to look at. They were undersized, with a ragged build and a dejected appearance. Their small heads, which drooped sadly, were the only suggestions of beauty and intelligence about them. These were molded in lines as delicate as a doll's face, with widespread and bulging eyes, that peered from half-shut lids. Their front legs came out close together from a narrow chest, and the hind ones were spindly and ill shaped. These two peculiarities were the principal qualities which gave them such wonderful action as cow ponies. The closely placed front legs served as a delicate pivot to whirl suddenly one way or the other, and the crooked hind ones served as a spring cushion when making a sudden stop. The deep and narrow chest harbored great lung development and breathing power, which gave them added stamina. They were not speedy by any means, but they always came in at the finish of any endurance test. The role of destiny which the Spanish pony was to play in the development of a great industry was already shaped for him when the first Americans started rounding up cattle, but no one knew it at that time.

In spite of the Spanish pony's downcast appearance, no animal ever lived which was more alert. Three hundred years of wild life, where he moved about in constant danger and was compelled to carry on an endless fight for existence against the forces of nature and all other animals, including those of his own race, had whetted his senses to a razor sharpness. His sight was as keen as an antelope's; his hearing sharp as a deer's and his smell acute as a bloodhound's. What he lacked in speed was made up in quickness, and he had the agility of a mountain sheep.

It is claimed by some authorities qualified to speak upon the subject that the bucking horse is peculiar only to America. The trait was acquired as a defense against the mountain lion, which was his deadliest enemy. It was the habit of those fierce cousins of the tiger to lie in wait upon a tree limb around the watering places and spring upon the back of an unsuspecting yearling or colt. The flesh of a young horse was the choice food morsel of those crouching, clawing and vicious beasts, who killed their prey from its back by crushing its neck in powerful jaws. The animal that was able to fling the assailant away before receiving the fatal stroke was the one that survived.

Whether this theory is correct or not, it is a known fact that those wild horses when cornered would fight desperately with every means at their command. They could bite with the ferocity of a crocodile, kick with the force of a sledge hammer blow, and, using their front feet, they could strike with the sureness of a grizzly bear. When time came for them to be tamed and broken for service, they made no distinction between man and their other foes. A line from an old poem which purports to delineate some of Satan's nefarious work and which was widely recited among cowboys fifty years ago, may serve to illustrate the point with reference to the wild horse. It says in part:

"He poisoned the legs of the centipede — and put seven Devils in the broncho steed."

As was the case in many other phases of his newly adopted trade, the American cowboy had yet to learn to ride. He had plenty of material at hand for practice, but to this day the art has never been fully mastered. Many riders have became experts in their line, but none has ever reached the state of perfection. Proof of this can be seen at nearly any rodeo performance when a professional rider is unbalanced by some peculiar twist or convolution of his mount and is thrown to the ground just as ungracefully as an amateur.

It took a good man to keep his seat aboard a bucking, bawling, whirling horse when the animal was wound up to full capacity. Those old Spanish ponies could arch their backs into a hump like the curve of a hoop and, with heads thrust between front legs, there was very little left for a man and his saddle to rest upon. When they went aloft and came down, all four feet would be bunched together in a space no larger than could be covered with a wide-brimmed hat, and, by reason of wheeling and weaving and bouncing here and there like a rubber ball, it was hard indeed for a rider to keep his seat. This high-flung and strenuous action lasted until the rider was either thrown or the animal had become exhausted and was forced to let up.

The average Spanish pony never became fully gentle and safe for a novice to ride. He performed his work willingly, in a manner to command pure admiration from his rider, but upon the spur of the moment some unlooked-for incident might touch him off. The next instant, his admiring rider might either be trying desperately to retain his seat in the saddle or be stretched upon the ground. Many a man has been caught unawares by such a sudden splurge and unseated before he had a chance to show his skill and prowess as a rider.

As quickly as a broncho horse became tractable to hackamore rein, he was considered broken, but that did not stop his bucking by any means. Even so, when he was put to work upon the roundup or trail, he seemed to take to cattle herding by natural instinct. His calm nature and watchful disposition especially fitted him for the purpose. With that delicate head carried at an even level and his intelligent and watchful eyes upon the cow he might be driving, he was able to make a quick but careful selection of the spot where he placed his feet at each step. He would skim at full speed over rough ground strewn with rocks and ledges or criss-crossed by ditches and gullies when it seemed impossible to keep footing. He seldom if ever stumbled or fell.

From experience, cowmen learned that it was highly important for a horse to keep his head and neck on level. He could watch both the ground and the cow better that way. A bridle bit when placed in a young horse's mouth often cut and bruised it to such sensitiveness that he would flinch and throw up his head in reaction to the pain when the bridle reins were tightened. Because of this condition, a bit was never placed in a horse's mouth while he was being broken. Indeed, some men never allowed a cowboy to ride one with bridle and bit until he had been ridden a full season with a hackamore. The Mexican hackamore with its drooping noseband was the only instrument of restraint that a prospective cow pony ever knew until he became thoroughly guidable and submissive to the rein. He was then considered hackamore or bridle wise, and a bit could be placed in his mouth. Thus, a cow pony worked while he received his training, and every precaution was taken to prevent the distraction from his work by a sore mouth. Not only was it essential for a horse to keep his head low and eyes watchful while following a cow, but he also needed to watch where he was placing his feet. A man's life ofttimes depended upon the clear-footedness of his horse.

As the cattle business grew in scope, the need for cow ponies grew with it. Within a few years after cross-breeding was started, there was a plentiful supply at hand. It has been said that at one time the price of a horse was on a parity with the cost of a pair of shoes. Some cowmen found it profitable to raise their own supply of saddle stock and sell off the surplus or those unfit for their needs, while others bought theirs in the open market. This latter course was followed more or less by the larger outfits, who made a practice of buying unbroken geldings of mature ages each year to replenish the supply. Each outfit wanted to break, or supervise the breaking of, its own horses. Cow ponies were needed solely for working cattle and were of such vital importance that no man wanted to chance their future to irresponsible hands. Many a good and promising horse has been ruined by improper breaking.

For a number of years the regular cowboys broke the wild horses. After a time, this practice was abandoned. There were two reasons for the change in policy. While most cowboys could ride well enough to hold their jobs, it was not everyone who cared to break horses along with his regular work. It required much more physical exertion and carried extra dangers as well. Any man who made a practice of breaking horses at some time or another reached the stage in life when he acquired a mortal fear of a bad one. Then, having wild horses in an outfit frequently disturbed things and delayed the program of working cattle, which was the primary object. The outgrowth of the horse-breaking problem resulted in the creation of another branch of the industry. This led to an entirely distinctive personnel when the professional broncho buster came upon the scene.

At first the professional horse-breakers were recruited from the ranks of cowboys. Since the occupation involved extra hazards, it naturally commanded a higher rate of pay. This attracted a more daring and reckless class of men. There was also more independence among bronco busters than among ordinary cowhands. Their business relations with the outfit were on a contractual basis of so much money per head for each horse broken and turned into the outfit for use. Their board was furnished at the ranch, and they were given the use of corrals, and the gentle horses necessary for handling the wild ones. There was no set and stipulated time for completion of the job, and they were free from discipline and orders, except for being continuously under the watchful eye of the boss, who made it his business to see that they did not abuse and mistreat the young horses. If the weather was inclement, there was no one except themselves to say whether or not they should work a certain day.

The bronco busters usually went in pairs, so they could assist one another in the strenuous work. They traveled from one job to another on the various ranches. They put in the entire season at their profession. In time, a line of distinction was drawn between the professional horsemen and ordinary cowboys, which was widened more or less by resentment and jealousy.

Ordinary cowboys regarded the professional bronco busters as incompetent and lazy, because they followed only one line of the great industry. They were accused of seeking the comparatively easy life of the ranches, where there was no night work, and where they enjoyed shelter from the weather. On the other hand, the bronco busters held the common cowboy in more or less contempt. They argued that cowboys were afraid of the bad horses, which fact was the only reason the professionals had a job. This controversy remained a hot issue as long as the open-range horse and cattle business flourished. As far as anyone knows, it is still unsettled.

As the horse business expanded, the two factions grew farther apart. In time, the personnel of cattle and horse outfits had little in common and bore little or no relationship to each other. This was especially true when the great horse ranches of the extreme Northwest were in operation during the latter part of the nineteenth century. In certain sections of this area, the range was well adapted for horse raising and not for cattle. In this region, men learned the trade of horse handling, which included breaking the wild ones, and followed it for years without ever turning a range cow around or running a brand upon a single calf.

Proof of their unfamiliarity with cattle was seen many times when hired hands of the great horse ranches decided for one reason or another to change occupations and try cowpunching. Now and then, one or more former horsemen drifted down into the cattle ranges of Montana, Wyoming or the Dakotas, and their ignorance of cattle lore was plainly apparent. They could not rope a cow by the head — much less by the feet. In many cases they were unable to find, and rope, their own saddle horses in the corral. They could not read brands with any certainty, and it was a common thing for one to become lost while riding circle and wander around for hours before locating the roundup. They were as green about cow work as a farm boy from the East, and yet, they were complete horse masters. As the saying goes, they could ride a streak of greased lightning — once they got a saddle on it.

It required many and many horses to mount the men who made up the widely flung cow outfits of America. From the Gulf to the Canadian border — from the Missouri to the California mountains, thousands of men rode tens of thousands of horses on the wide roundup circles and over the long trails. The nature of the work demanded hard riding, and a horse could stand only so much. It frequently happened that one man would ride two or three horses down in a single day. The work was so strenuous that it took days for one animal to recover from such strenuous exertion, and, for this reason, it took several horses to mount one man. There were no supplemental rations of strong feed available, and the riding was done "on the grass."

The number of horses varied with the class of work and the conditions of the country. It is obvious that in trail work, where the movement was of a more leisurely nature, fewer would be required than were needed to carry a man over the long distances covered in making the roundup circles. From seven to ten head per man might be called a fair average. When the first herds were bunched together upon the Texas prairies, it is doubtful if any one man was assigned more than three of four head for his own use. Later, when the business was expanded and became more systematized, the importance of keeping a man well mounted was demonstrated, and the number was allotted according to the need. In Montana, where the last great roundups were staged and where romance and color of the industry came to its untimely end, it was common to see one man with as many as fifteen head of saddle horses in his individual string. There were times when three hundred or more horses could be counted in the *remuda* of a single outfit.

Contrary to what many writers of Western fiction seem to believe, mares and stallions were not employed as cow ponies. Some cowmen used them to a limited extent for ranch work, such as line and fence riding, but they were never found in the *remuda* of a trail or roundup wagon. They served their main purpose as breeding stock, and they were left running loose upon the range. Stallions were notorious for their vicious fighting qualities and they were extremely jealous of all male specimens of the breed. Even the gentle and tractable gelding was not immune from their wrath. With his superior strength, it would be possible for a lone stallion to maim or cripple a large number of saddle horses during a single night. It would not take long for one of them to put an entire *remuda* out of commission. For the reason of keeping down disturbances, mares were not used. While the sex impulse among geldings lay dormant, it was never entirely subdued among some. It can readily be seen the fights and disturbances that would follow should one or more female species be turned loose among some two or three hundred head of them. Horse wranglers of large cow outfits have strict rules governing such matters. No stallion or mare was allowed among the *remuda* while either upon the roundup or trail.

When a string of horses was assigned to a man, they were his own property to all intents and purposes. As long as he worked for the outfit, his trusteeship was inviolate and respected by all. It was considered a gross violation of ethics — and cowboys stood firmly on ethics and ceremony — for one man to ride another's horse without permission. Only in a case of extreme emergency would the boss of an outfit, or even the owner, break the rule, and then an explanation was in order. At one time it was permissible for the men to trade horses among themselves, but in most outfits this practice came to be prohibited. It proved out that shrewd bargainers often turned up with all the best horses while the less astute were reduced almost to the state of walking. When the bronco busters turned in a string of what they called "broke horses," these were apportioned among the men according to their needs.

It was customary for a cowboy to secure permission to break out during the off season one or more young horses that had struck his fancy. In this manner it was possible for him to eventually be riding a string of his own training. If one proved unsuitable, it would be turned into the *remuda* and another secured in his place. In this case the utmost care was followed in breaking, and if one exceptionally useful and outstanding animal was turned out, the cowboy felt that all his efforts had been abundantly rewarded. A favorite animal was guarded with intense jealousy and woe unto the man who rode him without first securing permission to do so. A cowboy loved a good horse, and he would go to any means to retain his trusteeship. When the boss of a certain ranch in Texas was ordered by the owners to proceed to their Colorado ranch and bring a hundred saddle horses with him, his heavy hand fell upon a favorite one which had been broken out and ridden by a sixteen-year-old boy. This boy followed the herd for seventy-five miles and in the night he stole the animal away just like a common thief and returned to the ranch with him.

It is not known at just what period during the development of the cattle business that men discovered the adaptability of the Spanish pony to work cows. Long before the English-speaking settlers came to Texas, Indians had trained their horses to the highest degree by chasing buffalos. No doubt the Mexican ranchers were the first to train horses in cow work and then they passed this information on to the Americans. While the

American cowboy eventually came to excel his Spanish-speaking contemporary in most phases of the calling, much knowledge of handling cattle came from the latter in the beginning. Mexicans had cow-herding down to a practical working basis long before any of the great herds were formed north of the Rio Grande. Therefore it is probable that the Mexicans were the first to learn that the Spanish pony possessed a natural desire and instinct to follow a cow as diligently as a hound follows a rabbit trail. He was encouraged in this inclination by his masters. Experiments proved that he worked best with the least restraint and guidance. All he needed was a free rein, and he improved his style by practice.

It is difficult to render a comprehensive outline of the qualities of a cow pony. Words are inadequate to give a full and clear description. The intelligence and zeal he displayed in this principal role of his useful life is unbelievable. His extreme quickness and agility were the principal factors in this trying and strenuous work. No cow could stop suddenly enough and dodge away quickly enough to escape. From a gait of running at full speed, he could come to a sudden stop within a single bound. His flexible hind legs absorbed the shock as softly as a cushion, while his rear haunches settled almost to the ground. He could spring away from that position instantly in pursuit of a cow, and he often turned so short and low upon a side that the rider's boot heel marked a streak in the dirt.

In spite of his deficiency in speed and build, he was endowed with the mental alertness and physical quickness of a cat. All of these powers he brought into diligent use while going about his favorite task of working cattle. Of all the higher bred animals that have been raised since his time, none has proven his equal in this particular phase of work. When the Spaniards carelessly scattered the seed of wild mustang horses in America four hundred years ago, no one dreamed of the important role they were to play in later history. It is as though a Divine Providence placed them for a single mission on earth in which they were able to perform so nobly.

It took years of hard work by the horse and patient training by its owner to bring the cow pony to a fine point of proficiency. Some learned quicker than others, and it was not difficult for a cowman to detect the most promising ones by their zeal. As each animal was subjected to his daily work, he grew in wisdom and learned the finer points of his task at hand. A finished cow pony was seldom turned out under four years of work and training.

Much can be said for the old cow pony and still never tell the whole story. He holds a sacred place in the memory of those who knew him best. Many a gray-haired man who rode the early cattle trails has a vacant yearning in his heart for another ride on him, but the wish will never be realized. The genuine cow pony has gone — never to return. He has fulfilled his mission and passed into history with only a memory of his glorious feats left behind. He would be of little use if he were still in existence today. Cattle are gentle and much easier handled than when they ran wild and unhampered. They are kept in small bunches, fenced inside pastures, and they come in contact with men nearly every day. When they are separated, the work is done inside corrals by men on foot, and almost any kind of an old plug horse will do to round them up.

In the old days great roundups were made by hard-riding men, who covered wide areas in order to bring the wild cattle together. Separating was done by one or more cowboys mounted upon their favorite cutting horses, who rode into the herds of restless milling cattle amid clouds of dust, to cut out the desired ones one by one. With heads low and eyes flashing, those cutting horses would duck and dodge with perfect coordination. In the vernacular of the cowboy, they could stop and turn on a silver dollar and give you back ninety cents in change.

Long before changing conditions and methods of handling cattle were curtailing the need of good cow horses, the original strain was being absorbed by cross-breeding with other and better graded stock. It was discovered, however, that when the lowly Spanish pony was bred up to a certain stage, he lost much of his usefulness as a cow horse. The first two or three crosses with better-blooded animals made a decided improvement. The cross-breeding gave him more size, and bone and speed without detracting from his other qualities. He was still a good cow horse and kept his eyes and his mind riveted to his work. He would last longer because of his increased size and strength, but too much breeding proved to be detrimental.

The main quality of a cow pony was his calmness and his disposition to keep his head down and a close watch upon the cow and the place where he was to plant his feet. The hot blood of the race horse with which he was generally crossed had a tendency to make him abandon this most important trait. The thoroughbred race horse is a proud animal, much of which is reflected in his stately carriage. His head is carried high and his thoughts are inclined to soar aloft with his shining eyes as they look upon distant horizons. It is not for him to be satisfied with the dejected appearance of a lowered head, nor be content to follow a cow. It is his natural instinct to run ahead and lead the way and never follow. He is easily excited and under stress and pressure is inclined to forget the importance of selecting a firm and safe spot to set his feet while running. In his reckless and headstrong impulses, he has been known to stumble and fall without apparent cause or reason. On the other hand the Spanish pony was not so speedy, but he had that instinctive caution to select a firm spot of ground to place his feet. Thus it is only natural that, by cross-breeding, much of the hot-blooded pride of the thoroughbred eventually would be instilled into the Spanish pony, and rob him of certain qualities.

Not all the horses broken out and trained for cow ponies were satisfactory. Some were entirely unfit and others were mediocre. The unfit were soon disposed of, and the common ones used for less exacting work. A large majority of the huge numbers that were broken and put to work made good and useful animals, but a very small percentage of them ever reached the fine state of perfection of a cow horse. An outstanding cutting horse was a rarity among many. If all of them were added together the sum would be very small indeed when compared to the total number of horses that were employed during the era of range cattle prominence. It would be safe to say that not one out of every five hundred ever made a first-class cutting horse. Many cowmen lived their lives without ever owning one, and many a cowboy worked through the last twenty years of the nineteenth century when the industry reached its crescendo without ever riding one. Every cowman cherished the hope that some day he might uncover one of the prized possessions among his saddle horses, but few ever realized that ambition. Now they are gone forever.

Nothing short of patient training and hard work ever developed a first-line cow horse. It would be safe to say that only a few were made after the turn of the century and none after the first decade. There has not been the work to train them, and the kinds of animals being bred today are not disposed to take the training. There are some men who might with all sincerity dispute this argument, but they would speak without full knowledge. There are men still living who have seen or ridden some of the best cow horses that ever looked through a bridle headstall, but none of them are under fifty years of age. There are others past thirty who have been engaged in the cattle business all their lives who do not know the qualities embodied in a first-class cow pony. They do not know what a good cow horse is, because they have never seen one. It is doubtful if there is a living man under fifty years of age who has had his boot heel jabbed into the dust while sitting upon the back of a whirling cow pony.

It is true that the best and most useful horses the world has ever known are being bred today. They have size and bone and speed that outranks the old time Spanish pony. One of these highly bred animals can carry a double load twice as far in a day. If matched against one another in a race, the result would compare with the fable of the tortoise and the hare. On the other hand, not one of them can ever equal the Spanish pony in the field of endeavor for which he was best fitted.

Speed and quickness plus endurance have always been the prime requisites of a cowman for his horses. When he started to improve the breed of his saddle stock, it was natural that he turned to a class of animals for cross breeding that embodied these qualities. From a cross of the Spanish pony with the thoroughbred, there has evolved a distinct strain of animals commonly called the quarter horse. There are various branches of this family, but the breed is not recognized as pure, and it is not listed in the *American Stud Book*. However, the quarter horse is a useful animal, and it is claimed by his sponsors that he comes close to embodying all the qualities of the Spanish pony, plus size and bone and speed. If properly handled, and if the work were here to train him, no doubt this animal would make a creditable showing as a cow horse. This does not mean that he would rank along with the Spanish cow horse. With all due respect for the opinions of the quarter horse backers, there is no horse today that can equal the feats performed by those old cutting horses of fifty years ago.

The principal defect of the quarter horse as a cow pony is his thick build and heavy body upon slender legs. While his straight and shapely legs are embodiments of distance, reach and speed, they do not have the spring that is necessary to make sudden stops with ease. It would be extremely tiring for him to support his weight during quick turns and sudden stops upon unyielding legs and delicate ankles. The Spanish pony's hind legs were crooked and ill shaped, but springy as those of a jack rabbit. They formed a resilient cushion for his weight, and he could whirl and dodge without bringing undue strain upon them.

There are some who dispute the claims of the quarter horse fanciers and lean to other breeds as the ideal. The divergent trends of thought are fostered by men well qualified to speak upon the subject. The controversy is of long standing and seems no nearer settlement than when it was first started. It all boils down to individual opinion and each man is entitled to his own. All are correct in their claims for good horses, and the new breeds are suitable for working cattle of this day and time. But they are wrong when they set forth the claim that their favorite breeds could equal the Spanish pony in working cattle when cattle were wild and hard to control. If the work were here to train them it is doubtful if either of the cherished breeds could ever learn to dodge and whirl and make the sudden stops so necessary in a prize cutting horse. It would be safe to risk a bet that none of them could turn low enough for the rider's boot heel to gouge into the dirt, nor stop with a suddenness that would set their haunches upon the ground.

CHAPTER ELEVEN
THE COWBOYS

SOMETHING has been said about different personalities who had a hand in shaping the course of the cattle business. The names of a few individuals who played an outstanding part have already been mentioned. There are many others worthy of that distinction, but to compile them all would make the list read like a directory. Those whose names have crept into this record were leaders in their field, but they were the owners of the cattle that other men handled. Now the time has come to introduce the cowboys who did the actual work.

One striking side of the many interesting elements that went to make up the cattle industry was the kind of men who were attracted to it. No undertaking in world history ever gathered such a unique and picturesque set of characters. No single class of men was ever enshrouded in such romantic and glamorous atmosphere as were those who rode upon the wide roundup circles and followed the great herds over the trail. No group of men and their deeds ever laid a foundation for as many written pages of literature and song as the cowboys. None was ever more deserving of the glory that clings to their memory. No more courageous and daring and resourceful and loyal body of men was ever assembled in a single private purpose. Requirements of their trade demanded all these qualities, and any man without them never reached the station of a cowboy.

It has been truly said that "cowards never started, and the weaklings never got there." To this quotation could be added another appropriate phrase — the unfit could not stay. There was skill and technique that went with a cowboy's trade, and not everyone who came along could master it. Groups of men have been brought together in other undertakings, but they all had their quotas of weaklings and cowards and misfits. None of these could survive among the men who carried on the far flung cattle industry. One may have had no fear of any other man while, at the same time, he would not be willing to risk himself upon the back of a plunging, side-swiping, end-turning, bucking bronco. Another may have been fearless while riding his charging horse upon the insecure footing of a hillside, and still cringe before the tongues of forked lightning licking out at him during a thunderstorm in the darkness of night, while trying to soothe a herd of wild and restless Longhorns. To be acceptable as a cowboy, one had to overcome all these fears, and many others.

It took courage for a man to brave the known dangers and venture into an environment where he might be called upon to fight for his life at any time. In the early days there was the mortal threat of Indians, besides the ever-present danger of a personal encounter with a fellow worker, or other desperate characters who had been attracted to the country by the flow of easy money. Where such belligerent classes as sailors, miners and lumberjacks settled their disputes with fists and clubs, cowboys and other men of the West resorted to guns when involved in an altercation. Thus a fight on the cattle range or in any of the small cowtowns scattered over the wide prairies usually meant a killing, and no coward had a stomach for subjecting himself to this constant risk by taking up the life of a cowboy. There were no convenient police or other officers to protect a timid person from an audacious one, and each man had to be more or less a law unto himself. It is true that many men lived their lives on the cattle range without ever firing a gun at anyone or without ever being shot at, but the chance of such an encounter was ever present, and the early-day cowboy realized this and was ready to face it.

It took courage and determination in other ways for a man to qualify as a genuine cowboy. No coward would pull himself hand over hand down a tightly drawn rope before dawn toward a fighting, kicking, pawing horse on the other end, to saddle him. It took courage for one to step into the stirrup and seat himself upon the humped back of that same horse, with no bars of restraint between them and the wide, wide world except a pair of slender bridle reins. It took courage for a man to ride in the lead of two thousand stampeding wild steers over treacherous and uncertain ground in the dark of night, with heavy raindrops slashing at his face. All this was done many times when there was no guiding light except blinding flashes of lightning that rolled along the ground in fireballs, and played upon his horse's mane and ears as it scorched the hair. It took courage to face these and many other dangers that one learned about at first hand when he saw them take their toll of human lives.

But personal bravery was not the only requisite for a good cowboy and a misfit was out of place beside him. There were plenty of men with courage to spare who could never master the intricacies of the trade. A passable cowboy had to learn them all and be able to perform when the occasion arose. He had to be able to shoot, ride, rope, and read brands and be ready to do hundreds of other things on the spur of the moment. He had to be a close student of nature, and learn the habits and traits of animals, and read the signs in the skies and all the records of nature spread around him. There were times when his life depended upon this knowledge. All these things and many more a cowboy had to learn, as his trade was not one that called for specialization.

It is true that some would excel others at different phases of the calling, but each man had to be able to perform all tasks because he might be faced with a problem involving any or all of them at any time, day or night. All men felt the necessity of being a good shot and quick on the draw in case of a fight; the lapse of a second might mean the difference of life or death. Naturally in a conflict between two men, one was bound to win and the other lose, but that is how a man had to meet the test. In order to stay on the cattle range, each individual had to believe in his own ability to take care of himself; and he had to have the courage to stand by his own convictions. Thus, with the skill required to carry on the trade, and with the known dangers that beset it, there is ample reason for the belief that the industry attracted only courageous and resourceful individualists.

This does not mean that all cowboys were men of great stature and brawn and muscle. Indeed, the contrary is true. Once again, individual qualities assert themselves and make a conspicuous distinction between the cattle industry and other callings. A cowboy's work was done by skill and finesse to a much greater degree than by main strength and awkwardness. The cattle range is one place where a small man had an even break and could hold his own with a larger one. It has been truly said that the Creator made some men decidedly larger and stronger than others, but a man by the name of Colt came along and put them all on equal footing when he invented the six-shooter. Fighting was done with guns, and it was not the question between two belligerents which was the larger or stronger, but the outcome of an encounter hinged on which one could whip his gun to a level the quicker and pull the trigger. A small man is generally agile and quick in his actions, and for this reason he was at no disadvantage in a fight.

It would take a very large and strong man indeed to turn a running horse end over with the loop of his rope upon the plunging front feet by pure muscular strength, but the knack of catching an animal off balance with feet in the air and making a sharp pull upon the rope at that instant could be learned just as well by a small man as a large one. The act of riding a bucking horse was not done by brute strength, but an expert rider learned the fine art of perfect balance, and how to harmonize the motion of his body with that of the horse. It takes little physical exertion to cast the loop of a rope from the back of a horse upon the horns of a running steer, or upon the front feet of an animal in a corral, but deftness and exact timing are the secrets. Thus, it is plain that cowpunching was one form of strenuous, outdoor life where a small man was not handicapped by size. All he needed was adaptability at learning the tricks of the trade and the courage to put them into effect.

As the cattle industry spread and developed, cowboys were gradually molded into a caste of their own. Under their system of individual rights, a most rigid code of ethics was formed and guarded jealously. Each was considered to be the master of his own destiny without benefit or interference from any other. A man's private life was all his own, and it was seldom, if ever, a topic for discussion. Violation of this code usually laid the foundation for a fight.

In general, cowboys were men of few words, and certain precepts were followed, but not discussed. For example, a man never spoke with reverence about his own family. That would have been a waste of words and to do so would breed a doubt as to his motive. It was understood that a man's mother was all-high in his respect, love and worship, and such being the case, why talk about it? Personal questions were never asked, and if one volunteered such information he received respectful attention unless he talked too much. A voluble and lengthy discourse about intimate affairs was bad taste and unbecoming to a gentleman. Private affairs were considered inviolate and duly respected, but if one showed no respect for them himself, he was judged unfit for cowboy society.

Cowboys were the most overworked and the least paid for their time and talents of any class of men in the whole world. There was great physical risk to their calling and a required skill that took many years to learn. The amount of knowledge that a cowboy crammed into this head was tremendous, and he was frequently called upon to make important decisions and act upon the spur of the moment. There were no rules or references at hand for consultation in solving a perplexing problem, and his memory and ability to make instant decisions were his only guide.

In spite of the miserly wages that a cowboy received for his long hours of faithful and dangerous work, he was by no means a vassal slave. He was the proudest, the most independent, the most self-reliant creature that ever tramped the face of the earth. He was the undiluted personification of freedom and was jealous of his rights. He would stand on principle and die for it if called upon to do so. He put in long hours of dangerous work amid any and all kinds of weather without a murmur of complaint, but he never stooped to the level of menial servitude. He was a gentleman on horseback, cheerfully performing such duties as befitted a man of his station, but he drew the line at drudgery or manual labor. He would harness and hitch a team of horses to the chuck wagon, but he would not drive the wagon. He would ride into a motte of timber and drag up firewood with a rope to the horn of his saddle, but nothing short of dire emergency could induce him to chop up the wood. That was the work of the cook or horse wrangler, who, according to a cowboy's standards, were far below him in the social scale. It would have been a gross insult for his employer to order him to plough a field.

One of the strictest codes maintained by a cowboy was loyalty to the brand which he represented. Although he might be underpaid and overworked, as long as he rode an outfit's horses, he was for them with all his mind and body. He would fight for his employer at the least provocation when he knew his only reward would be the knowledge that he had been true to his creed. In many ways the employers reciprocated with fidelity. A cowboy always had the comforting knowledge that he was protected from outside harm. If he became sick or injured, all doctor bills were paid and his wages ran on just the same. He had a welcome home at the ranch during sickness and convalescence. Frequently his escapades of celebrating too liberally in town got him into trouble with the law-enforcement officers, but he rested secure in the knowledge that loyal friends and the outfit's money stood firmly behind him in the hour of need.

If the average cowboy was reticent among those of his own sex, he was absolutely tongue-tied in the presence of women. The only ones he ever encounterd were those he met in the cowtowns, or the small farming settlements adjacent thereto. In the days when cowpunching was in its zenith there were no women to be found on the ranches. No self-respecting man would subject a feminine member of his family to the drudgery of ranch life. No ranches of those days were equipped with conveniences, and the loneliness would have been maddening. The men who did the work were out with the roundup or trail wagons for long stretches, and the time they put in around the ranches during the spring and summer and fall months was negligible in comparison. The only reassurance a woman would have had in such a situation was her personal safety. After the Indians had been disposed of and quartered on their reservations, there was not the slightest danger to an unprotected person on the cattle ranges. In later years, when some women took up abode in the scattering ranch houses, there was never a case of harm coming to one at the hands of those who rode the range.

Because they spent long periods with only men as companions, cowboys became woman-shy and ill at ease in the presence of one. Many went through life without marrying simply because they were too bashful to court the one of their choice and make the proper proposal at the proper time. Thus, with a man's natural longing for the companionship of a mate denied him, he eventually came to idolize women and worship them in his imagination. A strong code of respect for all women was developed — and maintained. No cowboy would stigmatize the name or character of a woman by word or act, because that was one of the unpardonable sins. The foundation for such a precept could be credited to early training, but its real strength came from concentrated determination of all parties concerned to uphold it.

Among all cowboys there was an inherent respect for, and belief in, the Deity. No matter what pattern of life a man on the cattle range chose to follow, the influence never departed from his trend of thought. Although praying was seldom ever practiced, the roughest and most hardened among the cowboys frankly admitted that a time would come when any, or everyone, would pray if he had a chance. Unfortunately too many were called upon to answer for their earthly deeds without an opportunity for repentance. Part of this attitude could be traced back to home influence, but there is still a stronger reason for those men who isolated themselves from all agencies of spiritual guidance to maintain a strong belief in the Almighty. Undisputed proof of such an existence was before them every day.

It became a part of a cowboy's trade to study nature in its primitive form. Much of his comfort, and frequently his life, depended upon such knowledge. He learned by close observation of celestial bodies and wild life to make a reasonably accurate forecast of the weather. He learned that animals were guided by an instinct almost as unerring as the fact that day follows night, and that each instinctive mood had a meaning. Some of these he could interpret, while others remained unfathomable. It was only natural that all these phenomena should open up his vision for thought and contemplation upon the mysteries of life. He knew that animals were devoid of reasoning powers, and there was no other answer for their unerring instincts except for an unseen, and unknown, force to be at work.

From necessity much of a cowboy's life was spent in the open without a roof to obscure his vision of the sky. He also spent many hours awake at nighttime, with no other companions about him than the animals which he controlled. The solitude of night seems to probe deeply into men's souls and bring out true and untarnished reflection. Therefore, it is no wonder that any man should be impressed when he has had the opportunity to observe the laws of nature at work and sees miracles that are performed around him day in and day out. When he has seen all this and had a chance to study and contemplate upon all the phenomena before him, he certainly would be a fool to deny the presence of a Supreme Being.

A cowboy's day was full of risks and dangers and it was strictly a young man's game. The life was too strenuous for one who had reached the age of prudent caution. It was seldom that any man past thirty years of age felt himself equal to all the hazards. The hours of work were long and trying and he subjected himself to the whim of the elements. The horses were bad and hard to ride, and soon came to be feared. Some men have been heard to remark that they would lie awake all night, dreading the horse they had to ride next morning.

This does not mean there was a quick turnover of all cowboys reaching a certain age. There was always less exacting work to be done, such as line riding and, after fencing became general, fence repairing, where gentler horses were at hand and the hours were much more regular and agreeable. In fulfilling these lighter tasks a man could enjoy the comfort of a warm bed under a roof every night. At a certain period, some quit the trade altogether, and found employment in livery stables which were common and plentiful in that day. Others went into business in a small way for themselves, while others made peace officers and some took up the profession of bartending or gambling in the saloons. Be that as it may, few, if any, stayed actively engaged at cowpunching for many years.

While most cowboys were of a serious frame of mind, they also had a sense of humor and their moments of levity. When no dude or tenderfoot was around to serve as a butt for their jokes, they played pranks upon each other. A dude was their choice victim, and those who stepped foul of a crowd of fun-bent cowboys were led through some novel and thrilling experiences. There were snipe-hunting expeditions, badger games and other jests conducted at the expense of some innocent novice. The most harrowing of them all was the crazy man prank.

This joke worked best at a wagon out on the range. It had to be pulled upon an unsuspecting stranger, because no man familiar with the ways of cowboys would ever fall for it. Upon the approach of a victim, the roughest and toughest looking man in the outfit would be chained to the wagon wheel. It would be explained to the visitor that the unfortunate man had suddenly gone berserk, and that was the only way to restrain him from committing violence. The subject's disheveled appearance would support such a fear. He would even foam at the mouth, the foam being induced by holding a small piece of soap between his lips and mixing it with the moisture. At a critical time, the subject would break loose and run after the visitor. No man could stand hitched with a bellowing maniac coming after him. He would either shoot or run, and some of the cowboys were always close enough to prevent a gun from being pulled. The incident always ended by the offending stranger's taking off across the prairie on foot.

Not all cowboys were good by any means. Many were bad and others were worse, according to our precepts and standards. Some of the most notorious outlaws that ever infested the West had their beginnings as cowboys. Train hold-ups, bank robbers, cattle and horse thieves, and even hired killers were recruited from the ranks. A common quality among them all was the lack of fear. None of those early-day cowboys was afraid of anything on earth, which is one explanation why the bad men of the West were so hard to subdue. All Western sheriffs were cognizant of these traits and knew that an outlaw seldom if ever gave up without a fight.

A famous sheriff in New Mexico, while preparing to go out and arrest a train robber he had located hiding in the vicinity, remarked that there was a five hundred-dollar reward for the arrest, but as for himself, he would rather give five hundred dollars than to go up against the outlaw. It took brave men to hold the office of sheriff in the cattle country, and they knew that no person or class held a corner on bravery.

In general, cowboys were just a reckless and impetuous lot with less regard for their own well-being than for others. Their chief form of amusement seemed to be the annoyance of sedate town people in general and local peace officers in particular. Racing their horses up and down the streets and upon the board sidewalks of cowtowns, with occasional blasts from their pistols to liven things up, was just innocent amusement to them. No harm was meant by such antics, but it cost many a thoughtless youngster his life. The town marshals were not the kind of men to take unnecessary chances, and they knew that their lives often depended upon their ability to get in the first shot.

The peace officer's lot was a hazardous one, and the longer one stayed on the job, the colder and more calculating he became. His duties led him into many dangerous situations, and in too many instances he became a professional killer. This does not mean to imply that peace officers were not a necessary link in the preservation of law and order. Plenty of desperate characters rode their horses into the cowtowns to mix and mingle with other lawless elements who preyed upon all classes of society for their livelihood.

Cowboys were young and virile, and it is no wonder that after many months spent in the monotony of the roundup or trail drive, they sought relaxation in the most hilarious form that was at hand. In their quest for excitement, they had much aid and encouragement. The saloon and gambling houses and fancy women lived off the flow of money from the cowboy's pockets, and they strove to please the customers for a price. There was never a freer class of spenders than the cowboys and frequently their wild celebrations led them afoul of the peace officers.

Gambling was the chief form of entertainment in the cowtowns. The games ran wide open and in most cases without limit to the stakes. The entire proceeds from a herd of cattle have been known to change hands over a green-covered table at a single sitting. While the games ran wide open, without legal restraint or supervision, they were for the most part conducted on an honest basis. This was not altogether due to the average gambler's love of honesty, but there was another law governing his actions that was much quicker and more violent in its application than any court procedure. Fear of the victim's wrathful vengeance had a staying effect on a gambler's greed and served to keep the game straight. Cheating at cards was the lowest form of trickery and sudden death was considered a justified fate for one who indulged in such a practice.

This does not mean that all cowboys and cowmen put in their time in saloons, gambling and drinking and shooting. Indeed many of them shunned such places and the rowdy element as they would shun a pestilence, thoroughly convinced that they were truly agencies of the Devil. However, there were enough who did indulge to make a fearful noise. The only relation the good and the bad bore to each other was the fact that they all walked where they pleased, unafraid.

From the ranks of those ill paid and overworked men geniuses were made. The pattern of individualism was never cut from a broader cloth, and there has never been a field in the world where all men had such equal opportunity. As in all other walks of life, outstanding individuals forged ahead, and from these, range and trail bosses, and even cattle barons, were made. Although the school education of many was limited only to their ability to scrawl their names upon a document, yet great stores of knowledge were packed into their heads. To them the law of nature was an open book and they could foretell many events by observation just as accurately as a student could solve a mathematical problem.

Some possessed photographic minds and could picture a herd of walking cattle of two thousand head with their eyes shut. If any cattle had become lost during a stampede or from other causes, they could describe many of the missing animals. This ability was not acquired by any mystical insight, but it came about by close study and observation. They learned to know individual animals just as they knew men. They learned that when a herd of cattle became settled to trail routine, most of them held the same place in the line each day. It was not too difficult for one who had made a study of such things to ride alongside the herd and discover that certain animals were missing from their regular places.

But not all of those who mastered the arts of the trade made the best of their learning. Some were serious enough and attentive to business when work was at hand, but when relieved of responsibility, the desire for relaxation and frivolous entertainment outweighed all thoughts of preparing for the future. It is pitiful that many good men went down the hill of moral degradation and dropped by the wayside in a game that was too fast for a weakling to play.

At times a man may be excused for indulging in daydreaming or wishful thinking. The most impressive spectacle that one could imagine would be a grand parade of all bonafide American cowboys. It would include those who took part in the operations from the beginning, to the latter part of the nineteenth century. What a gathering it would be! Riding four abreast, the cavalcade would stretch for more than a hundred miles and the tramp of their cow ponies would sound like the roll of distant thunder running above the clouds. Like the vast herds of buffalo that roamed the western plains, the number would be almost uncountable. It would gather men from the blue waters of the Pacific to the mud banks of the Missouri; it would bring them from the steppes of Canada to the Rio Grande.

In the vanguard would be those intrepid souls who braved the Indian dangers of the Kansas Trail. Riding by their side would be the men of Goodnight and Loving who left their tracks across the high divides of West Texas and up through the Colorado mountains. With them would be John Chisum's men from New Mexico, with their high crowned hats and smoking guns. Farther back in the line would be the graceful Mexican vaqueros from Arizona and California, with their long ropes and undisputed skill in executing the *da le vuelta*. There would be the Canucks who drifted down from Canada to the Badlands of Montana, where they met the sunburned men from Texas. With them would be riding John Blocker's trail drivers, who were as familiar with the country along the Missouri and the Yellowstone as they were with their native land of the Brazos or Colorado.

There would be the thousands who rode circle in all the states making up the Great Plains area above the Cap Rock, along with the brush poppers from southern Texas with their short jackets and swinging *tapaderos*. Respectfully in the background and bringing up the rear would be those who took part in the closing episode at the dawn of the new century. No other gathering in the world's history could compare with it in color, and it would be more picturesque than the army of Alexander the Great. What a boon it would be to those proud cavaliers of the rope and saddle if they could be called back together and permitted to appear in a last grand finale.

The cowboy has passed into history, but his deeds and exploits will never be forgotten. He richly deserves all the glory that can be attributed to his memory. His station is still the goal of an adolescent's dream, and he still furnishes the foundation for countless written words of both prose and poetry. He has left his mark upon American history and culture just as plainly and just as permanently as though he placed it there with one of his red hot branding irons.

CHAPTER TWELVE

THE SUN HAS SET

FEW people realize the revolutionary changes that have overtaken the cattle industry. They could well be described as almost miraculous. There are men engaged in the calling at this time who do not comprehend the full measure of transition themselves. The greatest difference is between the animals that are being produced today and those which made up the first herds. There is a difference in the manner of handling them; a difference in the men and horses; a difference in the methods of financing the huge deals that are still being made. While the world has kept in close touch with developments in other affairs, this one great undertaking seems to have been overlooked by many people.

Details of the old style manner of handling cattle were far reaching and complicated. True and full knowledge of them could not be gained short of actual experience and observation. Most of those who knew all the ins and outs of the business were neither inclined nor educationally qualified to write extensively upon the subject. Few who attempt to tell about it now are able to speak with authority. Some glaring absurdities find their way into print.

Professional fiction writers for magazines and motion pictures seem to be the chief offenders. Most present-day editors appear to have relaxed their strict formula of demanding authentic matter in the material they publish, or else, they do not know any better themselves. Publications which have formerly been noted for exactness frequently run Western stories with incidents and characters entirely out of line with the times and customs they attempt to depict. Supporting illustrations are equally as bad. They often show characters dressed in a style of clothing and using paraphernalia that has only been adopted during the last few years. The cattle industry supplied enough romance and colorful characters that an unlimited amount of highly interesting fiction could be produced without resorting to gross misrepresentations and exaggerations.

Many people think that cattle are handled now as in the early days. There is little in the present system to compare with that in use fifty years ago. Like most other forms of progress, the change has been for the general good of all concerned. The meat-eating population of this land is blessed with a superior grade of beef. The men who produce it have a freer and fuller life. Cowboys are no longer called upon to battle hostile Indians or other lawless elements that formerly infested the ranges and cowtowns. They are no longer compelled to spend sleepless nights in the saddle, taking whatever the weather has to offer. While all of this has wrought a decided change for the better, it has robbed the calling of its romance and glamor.

The industry is conducted nowadays upon a well-organized basis. The same principles of modern business methods are applied as in any other industry. Means of financing are not like they used to be. At one time, money for handling cattle deals was as free as water in the rivers. Bankers who specialized in cattle loans risked huge sums of money upon the integrity of an individual. Cattlemen were long on honesty and courage, with supreme confidence in their own ability. Fortunes were made and lost quickly in those glorious days, but few failures could be laid to dishonesty.

Stocking of the Northwest ranges ushered in a grand era of trading. The decade following this epoch saw some of the most spectacular business deals that were ever consummated. Dodge City, Pueblo, Ogallala, Julesburg and Cheyenne all became great cattle trading centers. It was here that the trail men from the south met the range men from the north and carried on their transactions. It was the day when supreme confidence in the honor and integrity of mankind rode free and unhampered.

Thousands and thousands of cattle changed hands each year solely upon the word of the seller as to quality and condition. Equally as many others were sold and delivered into possession of the buyer with only a verbal understanding that the purchase price would be paid at some convenient and later date. The late John Clay, a former widely known cattleman and president of the Clay Robinson Live Stock Commission Company, told of a deal between himself and the late Murdo McKenzie, former manager of the Matador Land and Cattle Company of Texas, which is fairly illustrative. He stated that during the Eighties, he bought ten thousand two-year-old Matador steers for his Montana

TREAD OF THE LONGHORNS

ranch entirely on credit. There was no note or mortgage given, nor any form of a written agreement or promise to pay between them. There was a verbal understanding that the debt of more than a hundred thousand dollars would be paid some two years later when the cattle were sold. As a matter of record, they each entered the sum in their respective notebooks, and that was all.

We still have livestock speculators. The deals might involve huge sums of money, but they are not so spectacular as they once were. There were times when a trader bought thousands of cattle upon a shoestring with a courageous banker behind him. In those days cattle were counted out at so much per head, with the buyer risking his own judgment as to weights and market values. The present-day speculator buys his stock weighed over the scales at so much per hundred pounds, in line with market prices. Men and institutions who loan money no longer back up financial plungers in the livestock industry. Loans are advanced exclusively upon the ability of a person to meet payment of his note when due. It is a much safer and saner course to follow, but transactions of this kind do not carry the thrill that the great gambles for high stakes did in the days of long ago.

The most beneficial change that has come to the cattle industry is in the improved quality of beef that is being produced today. For many years, public-supported institutions have conducted far reaching experiments aimed at a better grade of meat at lower costs. Their efforts have produced remarkable results. In the old days Charles Goodnight and a very few other pioneers strove for the same purpose at their own expense. Few of the old time cowmen ever gave this phase of the industry any thought. Their main concern was to make a successful trail drive with their herds intact, and to secure ample water and grass enroute.

Now, many people who never saw a trail herd or a roundup are familiar with the technique of beef production. There are college professors, students and even Four H Club youngsters who know most of the answers. Many of them have never turned a cow around in their lives; some could not read a brand if it were drawn upon a piece of paper for them; some could not, as the saying goes, double up a rope and throw it in a well; and yet, they can discuss pound gainage and relative feed values with a better understanding than the average old time cowman who handled thousands and thousands of cattle during his lifetime.

There are still many so-called cowboys, and those who would like to be called cowboys. Evidence of this can be seen in almost any community west of the Mississippi nearly every day. Farm boys dismount from tractors and don a broad-brimmed hat, checkered shirt, and high-heeled boots and ride to town in an automobile for the night's entertainment. Cowboy regalia can even be seen on college campuses, worn by sons of men from all walks of life, including those interested in the cattle business. If an old time cowboy had a chance to change before appearing in public, he would never be caught in working clothes. The faddish desire to imitate a cowboy is indisputable proof of the influence he has wielded upon American culture.

There are many horses in use today which some people are pleased to call cow ponies, or cutting horses. For the most part they are well-bred and sightly animals, but there is little in comparison between them and the ones that made up the great *remudas* of the roundups and trail drives of fifty and sixty years ago. These animals are bigger and faster, but they do not have the inclination and wisdom to whirl and dodge and follow a cow like the ones that preceded them. Cow horses are no longer needed. There is not enough work to train them, and they are too highly bred and nervous to take the training if it was here for them.

There are still enormous ranches in operation that produce thousands of cattle each year, but they are managed in a different manner. The holdings are divided and subdivided into smaller units and the cattle are handled in smaller bunches. The round-ups are day-by-day affairs and are conducted from the comfortable quarters of a ranch house. Automobiles, and even dogs, are frequently employed in bringing the comparatively small bunches together in a roundup. Separation and classification of the animals is done mostly inside a corral by passing them through a chute with a dividing gate at one end. The gate is operated by a man perched on top of the chute, and it is not infrequent that he is protected from the sun's rays by an umbrella. It is no strain upon the imagination to see that an old time cowhand who prided himself upon his skill and the prowess of his cutting horse would snort with disgust at such a commonplace arrangement.

Back in the arid sections of the country where grass is thinner and immense acreages are needed to support a sizable bunch of cattle, some elements of the old style methods of handling them are in use. In a few localities, roundup outfits are pulled out for the purpose of working over the range, but the tenure of operation is measured in days as compared to months in olden times. Cattle are rounded up near long-established campsites where conveniences have been installed. Camp houses are available to shelter men from the weather, and small pastures are at hand to hold a herd and the few saddle horses overnight. Even upon the largest and most widely flung ranges there is little or no night herding of either saddle horses or cattle.

To these permanent roundup grounds or camps the calves are brought to be branded. In most cases, they are roped by the hind legs and thrown to the ground for this operation, but in others they are branded in an adjustable chute while standing on four feet. At any rate the work is done inside a corral by men on foot, while an old time cowhand did the same work upon the open prairie and mostly from the back of a horse.

Cattle are gentle in this day and time compared to what they were forty years ago. Constantly bringing them together in small lots for feeding makes them so. No finished animal ever goes to the slaughterhouse without having consumed more or less tamed or prepared feed. It is safe to say none go through a winter without additional feed served to them by the hand of man. All this tends to make any animal gentle, and as a result there is no need for skill and technique and trained horses to handle them. In the old days a beef steer lived his four to six years and went to his doom without ever tasting any other food than the natural grasses.

There are still a few men who are adept at many phases of the cowboy's trade, and who have kept alive some of the arts. Evidence of this can be seen at the many rodeo performances which have become an institution of the country. The difference is that the old time cowhands got their training in the course of everyday work, while rodeo performers specialize in certain branches of the calling. They have capitalized upon their knowledge and prowess, which has turned out to be a fairly lucrative business. Their average yearly income is far greater than the fondest hopes of an old time cowhand. Less general, all round ability is required for a successful rodeo performer than was necessary for a cowboy to hold a job in a first-class cow outfit fifty years ago.

A cowboy needed to do many other things besides rope and ride, and he had to do them under any and all conditions. If the weather was bad, he simply had to take it and hope for better times. A rodeo performer can specialize upon a certain branch of the trade and make a good living at it. He can enjoy the comforts of a house to live in, and he is never forced to perform under adverse weather conditions.

This is not intended to discount or belittle a rodeo performer's talents. Those who follow the circuits are good in their line, and they are fast. Most men who understand the skill and deftness displayed in his act will freely concede that a rodeo professional has reached a state of near perfection. On the other hand, many of the things included in a rodeo program are merely stunts designed solely for amusement of the spectators. As an example, the trick roping and riding were never a part of a cowboy's trade. Neither was the bareback horse and wild steer riding.

A cowboy did what was necessary in his line of work, but he never hunted for dangerous and unnecessary tasks. He would never ride bareback if he had a saddle. He never entertained the idea of riding a wild steer, because a horse was better. In the wild horse contests at a rodeo, the performers ride under serious handicaps which are imposed by the rules. A cowboy never subjected himself to such restrictions. Outside of a desire to put up what was called a clean ride, he had no further ambition toward showmanship. Riding a bucking horse was realized as a serious and risky piece of business and the ordinary cowboy did as little of it as he could get along with. Many an expert rider has been known to spend time and patience with a bad horse to keep him from bucking.

Riders at rodeos are recognized as being superb in their profession. On the other hand, a mere ride does not embrace all the difficulties. In a rodeo, while a horse is being prepared for riding, he is crammed into an enclosure so small that he is scarcely able to turn around. Willing hands place the saddle upon his back and tighten the cinches while the rider stands by at ease and supervises the operation. He even climbs upon the fence to mount, and when he is firmly seated in the saddle, the gates are swung open and the ride begins. He has no worries as to the course the horse may take, because the ground is perfectly level and the arena is hemmed in by an insurmountable fence.

An old time cowhand can conjure up a memory of an entirely different setup. He can remember the day when each man had a certain number of bad horses, or outlaws, in his string of supposedly gentle animals. The bad ones had to be ridden in their turn along with the gentle ones. He walked into a rope corral before the break of dawn amidst two hundred or more milling horses while he peered through the darkness trying to spot his choice of a mount for that morning. There were some fifteen or twenty other men coming and going to and from that corral upon the same mission. When his rope settled around the neck of his mount, he was led outside to be saddled. It may have been necessary to blindfold the horse, or tie up a hind foot, or stake both front feet to the ground with hobbles before the saddle was firmly set. Whatever measure it took, the cowboy did it alone. Other men were likewise engaged and no one had time to help the other. With the saddle securely cinched, the rider still had to get aboard. In many cases, this was considered the most difficult of all.

Few bad horses stood meekly while the rider mounted. Many were inclined to whirl away, trying to free themselves, ofttimes striking with their front feet, or kicking with their hind ones while the man clung precariously to the bridle check and saddle horn. When the rider's foot left the ground, the horse usually went aloft, while the rider tried to secure his seat in the saddle and the stirrup for his other foot. There was no selected spot for the performance. There were holes and gullies and ditches and hillsides for them to cross, and the horse didn't care. It was his object to unseat the rider. These are some of the hazards that an old time cowhand had to go up against.

Professional ropers who follow the rodeo circuits have never been surpassed in their chosen calling. The speed and deftness with which they rope and tie a calf is marvelous, but it is a different kind of roping. The old time cowhand did his throwing at any time or place and under all conditions. He had no level ground of an arena for his performances. Sometimes the chase led down steep hillsides and over rough ledges while his horse struggled to keep footing at a dazzling speed. Sometimes he plunged through brushy bottoms and while the horse jumped ditches or cactus bushes, the rider fended tree limbs from his face. This is part of the difference in rodeo roping and the style that was practiced on the open range.

Much credit for a rodeo performer's splendid work must go to his horse. On the other hand, it is doubtful if that same animal would be fit for any other phase of cow work. Like the roper, he has been trained for only one purpose. The present-day roping horse is hot-blooded and speedy and he takes to his work with zeal and eagerness. He is nervous and highly strung, a fact which is demonstrated by his actions while being restrained behind the barrier waiting for the flag to drop. Speed is an essential requirement for a rodeo roping horse. The lines of demarcation have been drawn so finely that a fraction of a second consumed in tying a calf may mean hundreds of dollars difference in prize money. The fractious disposition of the horse may also prove costly. If some mishap befalls him during a contest, he loses all sense of direction and responsibility and becomes unmanageable. In such an event, the roper can well count himself out of that particular contest.

In order to give more and better entertainment, a few stunts have been added to the list of cowboy acts. Trick roping and riding and bareback riding have already been dealt with. The most spectacular act of all is steer bulldogging. On its face, this has the appearance of genuine cow work, but outside of being dangerous and hard to do, it bears no relation to the trade. Twisting down a small animal such as a calf or yearling to be branded was as near as an old time cowhand got to bulldogging. No cowboy would have entertained the thought of riding alongside a speeding steer and flinging himself across its neck to grab the horns and wrestle it to the ground by main strength and awkwardness. He did his work by skill and deftness, and not by brute strength. Ropes were too plentiful, and he was too adept in their use to indulge in strong-arm tactics, such as bulldogging requires.

If some things have been added to the curriculum, others have been omitted. At least two which required considerable skill seem to have been lost. One was called going over the back and the other running across the leg. The latter might be construed to be one form of bulldogging, but it was performed more by technique than by physical exertion. It was done by a flanker on the branding grounds, running a calf across his leg and tripping it into a crushing fall. Going over the back meant riding alongside a running animal, spinning a loop over its back and picking up the front feet. The operation required a good horse, speedy work and exact timing. Whether these tricks are practiced back upon the ranches is not known, but they are never seen around a rodeo performance.

No more revolutionary change has come to any phase of the cattle business than the kind of ranches that now exist. To the first cowmen, a ranch meant simply the lands and house or headquarters where large numbers of cattle and horses were kept. It did not mean a farm, nor a garden spot, nor a country estate. A ranch embraced thousands and thousands of acres, but, generally speaking, it was known as the house or headquarters. The word stemmed from the Spanish *rancho,* which means a country home, but there was nothing very homelike about the early-day ranches in this country. At their best they were nothing to brag about. They consisted only of a shelter house where men had some protection from the weather, and that was all. They ranged in size from two-or three-room shacks to long rambling structures that could accommodate a larger number of men according to the needs.

In conveniences they were little or no better than a camp, and indeed, that was what many of them were called. Most had a range stove in one room for cooking, and a fireplace in the other for heat. In some, cooking was done camp style, upon the open hearth of a fireplace with the same utensils that were used upon the roundups or trail drives. Some had beds and others did not. While in winter quarters, most cowboys rolled their camp beds out upon the floor at night and rolled them up again next morning, the same as they did while out upon the range. During the season when cow work was running high, the ranch houses were for the most part deserted.

There were no women dwellers on the first ranches. Accommodations were non-existent, and the loneliness would have been unbearable. As time went on, and the radius of an outfit's operations was cut down, the ranch houses became more or less of a permanent abode. It became the practice for one or more men to remain at the headquarters all year, and in time the first women ventured out to endure the hardships. Even so, it was to be a long time before a ranch was fit for children. There were no medical or school facilities, and a family man engaged in ranching, either as an owner or employee, left his family in town.

From the time a woman set foot upon the ranch, there was a decided improvement in the surroundings. She swept the floors and hung curtains upon the drab windows. She nurtured flower beds around the porches and made a notable improvement in the quality of food. Running water inside a ranch house was unknown, but in time this seeming luxury was installed. Nowadays, a modern ranch has all the conveniences of a city dwelling, but it is a far call from its forerunners.

Just as a factory has come to be called a plant, so could a large ranch of this day be called a cattle plant. It has the buildings and other appurtenances to make it so. There is the huge structure of many rooms where the owner's family and their guests reside. There is the mess hall and its attachments, where the ranch hands secure their meals. There is a bunkhouse serving as sleeping quarters for the hired help, and in many cases the office is maintained in a separate building where the business affairs of the plant are conducted. The old time cowman kept his business affairs in his head. In addition there is usually one large barn and stable. There are machinery sheds, blacksmith shops, garages, and silos. Just as a large cow outfit in camp in the old days bore a resemblance to an Indian village, so does the modern ranch resemble a rural settlement, but the latter does not appear nearly so picturesque.

In the old days, and especially in the Southwest, where the weather was mild, there was, in addition to the ranch house, a corral for penning saddle horses. There were no barns, no sheds, nor any other structures except the building that served as living quarters for the men. In the Northwest, because of severe winters, there was usually a sod-covered shed large enough to stable three or four horses, flanked by a stack of hay. Where once it required a full day of steady riding on horseback or in a buggy to reach town over winding prairie roads, the same distance is covered nowadays in an hour by automobile over a graded highway. Indeed, some ranchers have gone the limit in modern transportation, and employ the use of an airplane in their travels.

If there has been a radical change in the ranches, horses, cowboys, and the methods of handling cattle, there has also been an equally drastic one in the class of cattle themselves. Formerly, a steer was not considered fully grown under four or six years of age. Even so, at full maturity, few of those animals ever attained a weight in excess of a thousand pounds. Now, it is common for a three-year-old steer to go to market weighing twelve hundred pounds or more. Improvement in the breed had a big effect in producing heavier animals and giving them a speedier growth, but a full ration of concentrated feed during their life is also an important factor in the rapid development.

Prices of cattle have always fluctuated more or less. At this time, they have soared to unbelievable heights. The value of common stock has advanced more than five-fold during the last fifty years, but the most drastic increase has been among the graded and pure-bred breeding herds. At an open, public auction sale conducted a short time ago, a single bull brought the grand price of fifty-two thousand dollars. It is within the memory of many men when this sum would have bought five thousand fair-grade steer yearlings, with some money left over. There have been times during the last fifty years when that amount would have been good for sixty-five hundred cows, or ten thousand calves.

However, these sky-high prices do not reflect a true condition of the cattle industry. For the most part, they are influenced by a few men whose major income is derived from other sources, and their cattle dealings are carried on simply as a side line or hobby. A few of them are what some people choose to call the *nouveau riche* with money to burn. Fifty thousand dollars for a pure-bred bull furnishes dazzling publicity, and if properly manipulated, it serves to reduce income tax payments. However, it is further proof of how the industry has influenced the general public and of man's desire to manage livestock and ride a good horse.

There are many excellent breeds of cattle in the country at this time, and as in other matters, opinions vary as to which class is the best. Naturally, climatic and other local conditions influence the choice, but judging by the large majority of cattlemen who are breeding Herefords, it is certain that this strain is the most popular. From the Mexican Gulf to the northern limits of grazing areas in Canada the familiar whiteface of the Hereford can be seen at any time or place. They thrive equally as well in the arid regions of the West, or in the humid, Blue Grass sections east of the Mississippi. They do well in the sultry, insect-ridden lowlands of the Gulf Coast and the Rio Grande, or in the high altitudes of the Rockies. They are thrifty and industrious in search of feed in places and at times where feed is scarce. They have stamina and will power to carry them through hard winters, and they are fairly prolific. Besides they make an excellent quality of beef.

The black species of hornless cattle still enjoy popularity. The strain was imported from the bleak highlands of Scotland, and their chief qualities are the absence of horns and ability to resist severe winters of the northern ranges. At one time, the black breeds threatened to become rivals of the Herefords, but as the years passed, Herefords took the lead and are now far out in front. No hardier class of cattle ever trod the open range lands of this country, and no better grade of beef was ever produced than the Aberdeen Angus or Galloway blacks. The main objection to them was that they did not cross well with other breeds and were not considered to be prolific under open range conditions. No doubt black cattle fanciers will dispute this statement, but such is the argument advanced by men who are qualified to speak upon the subject.

Besides the two above strains, there are many others. Shorthorns rank high in favor, but time has proven them to be most adaptable to small-scale production, where they can be given the best of care. There are two hornless breeds known as the Red Polls, and the Polled Herefords. Horns on cattle are considered a detriment at this day and time, and few ever reach the market without first being dehorned. They are inclined to injure one another with their horns when confined closely together in feed lots or railroad cars, and to prevent these injuries, they are relieved of their horns at an early age. In view of this, it would appear that the Polled Hereford would be the ideal breed, but so far they have not threatened to dislodge the straight Hereford from its throne of popularity.

There is one other newly created breed of cattle that may be worth mentioning. The oldest and most historic ranch of Texas has developed a cross between the Brahma imported from India, and the Shorthorn. The mixture was designed to be especially adaptable to the peculiar conditions in that part of the country. It is claimed that the new breed retains the heat and insect-pest resistant qualities of the Brahma while the Shorthorn strain gives it size and bone and quality of beef. Whether this is true or just a whim of its creator is not known, because the newly developed species has not stood the test of time. There certainly is nothing in the looks of the specimen to justify the opinion that it will supplant all other breeds in that section of the country.

Evolution of the cattle industry has greatly curtailed the use of horses in handling them. In some isolated cases and certain localities they have been eliminated altogether. Where in former years a cowboy was allotted from eight to fifteen head for his own mount, it is doubtful nowadays if more than three are ever assigned to one man at a time. Where once an outfit running fifteen or twenty thousand cattle employed some two or three hundred saddle and wagon horses, it probably gets along with a fourth of that number of saddle stock today. The wagon or work horse has come to be almost a thing of the past.

In the few remaining regions where cattle are still rounded up on the open range, at least twenty head of work animals would have been required at one time to freight supplies to a sizable ranch. Others would be needed to pull the chuck and bed wagons over the range from one roundup ground to another. Not one horse or mule is used for that purpose now. Automobile trucks roll quickly over smooth highways to trading centers for supplies, while roundups moving to and from various campsites have their equipment conveyed by truck over laid-out roads.

Comforts of these camps are better than those of the headquarters ranches fifty years ago. Present-day cowboys sit in chairs and eat their meals from tables instead of squatting around upon the ground with plates in their laps. They sleep on beds within the shelter of a house instead of upon the ground in soaking rains. If a herd of cattle happens to be on hand, it is safely confined in a small pasture while all hands sleep, instead of being held together by men riding around it all night. A telephone line connects some camps with the outside world, and most outfits carry a portable radio with them. In the old days news events were conveyed mostly by word of mouth by some rider passing from one cow outfit to another.

Trail driving is a lost art. A large percentage of cattle find their way to rail shipping points and market centers by truck. Few are ever located more than fifty miles from a railroad, and those that are driven move over a laid out roadway with convenient campsites and hold-over pastures en route. It is a rarity that a thousand head are ever brought togther in a single bunch.

Once in a great while some man decides to move a small bunch overland from one grazing area to another. It is a difficult undertaking because of farms and public roads lying across the way. It would be impossible to handle a large herd under such conditions, but with no more than a few hundred head, it can be managed. When such an event occurs, the public regards it as a novelty. Newspaper reporters give it wide publicity with exaggerated comments of their own thrown in for good measure. This is sufficient proof within itself that trail driving is a thing of the past. At one time hundreds of trail herds, with two or three thousand cattle in each, moved across the country and created no more interest than a truck farmer hauling a load of vegetables to market today.

During the run of a motion picture delineating a Western story, there are usually one or more camp scenes. Cowboys are shown comfortably reclining around the fire, picking at stringed instruments and indulging in song. What is supposed to be part, or all, of the herd is seen in the background, in close proximity to the camp, with the animals apparently charmed by the music. Such may be the case in present-day cow camps, but it is a long way from conditions that existed during the era that the picture is purported to represent.

The only time a herd ever got close enough to camp to be seen in a picture or listen to music was when it came that way in a stampede. In such an event, there would be no time for fiddling around with musical instruments, or singing, by the cowboys. They would either be taking to horse, or would be scrambling to get behind some object strong enough to withstand the rush and protect them from the avalanche of hooves that was coming toward them. In those days a cowboy spent very little time in camp anyway. He came in to get a change of fresh horses, or to eat, or to get what little sleep he could. When a man pounded the leather of his saddle from dawn to darkness, with a few extra hours thrown in for good measure while standing night guard, he had neither time nor inclination to indulge in song around camp.

Besides the fallacy of men taking it easy in camp, these scenes are always shown under ideal weather conditions. There is generally a huge moon floating among soft clouds, with a background of twinkling stars. Well, there were nights of this kind upon the trail, but there were other kinds also. There were times when a cowboy's life depended upon whether or not his horse stood up while he rode through pitch darkness ahead of twenty-five hundred stampeding cattle. There was no music except the beat of thunderclaps and the splatter of raindrops upon his hat and slicker. There were times when the world became suddenly illuminated by blinding lightning flashes, and a fiery tongue licked out to center upon some luckless victim and his horse, taking both of them into eternity.

The sun has been setting upon the glorious era of the old time cowman for many years and now it is down. Some men are still living who participated in the events of the last century, but few of them are engaged in the calling at this time. Unfortunately, many of those who once branded their calves by the thousands were reduced to extremely moderate circumstances before passing from the picture. Only a small prcentage were able to adjust themselves to changing conditions and keep their fortunes intact. Most of those who were far-sighted enough to invest their accumulations in land, managed to survive the financial catastrophes that have swept periodically over the cattle business. Time has proven that the man who owns his land, and raises his own stock, free from risky speculation, is almost bankruptcy-proof. It was the speculator gambling for high stakes who was doomed to financial failure.

There are a few men who have watched this metamorphosis of the cattle industry with regret. In their fading minds, they hold great and inspiring memories of which the world will never be apprised. No one but those who lived through these grand

and glorious times can paint a coherent picture of them. There is no substitute for actual experience. As time goes on and on, and those old cavaliers disappear from the scene, the knowledge they possess will be lost forever. There will remain only a few interested parties to write about them in a sincere, but feeble, attempt to perpetuate the memory.

ACKNOWLEDGMENTS

The author wishes to give credit to the following books which furnished factual material for a portion of this work:

The various writings of J. Frank Dobie; *Charles Goodnight,* by J. Evetts Haley; *Frontier Times* magazine, Editor, J. Marvin Hunter, Sr.; *Cattle, Cowboys and Rangers,* by William MacLeod Raine and Will C. Barnes; *The Chisholm Trail and Other Routes,* by T. U. Taylor; *The Great Plains,* by Walter Prescott Webb; *The Trampling Herd,* by Paul Wellman.

In addition to these written sources of material, the author has used freely the knowledge gained from the following individuals by word of mouth during his association with them:

His father, W. O. Gann, deceased, formerly of Leaday, Texas; Fogg Coffee and Bill Coffee, formerly of Leaday, Texas, deceased; Dan Molloy, of Edna, Texas; John C. Jones, of Coleman, Texas; H. R. Starkweather, formerly of Coleman, Texas, deceased; T. Joe Cahill and Charlie Embree of Cheyenne, Wyoming; Niel Boyle of Miles City, Montana, status unknown; Noah Ziegler, formerly of Oakley, Kansas, deceased; Will C. Gay of Coleman, Texas; Harry G. Hubert, of Junction, Texas; Bill Gatlin, formerly of Millersview, Texas, deceased; Howell Blackburn, formerly of Valera, Texas, deceased; Hi Farmer and Larry Thomas, of Miles City, Montana, status unknown; S. P. Woodward, formerly of Junction, Texas, deceased, and many others.

www.ingramcontent.com/pod-product-compliance
Lightning Source LLC
Chambersburg PA
CBHW030825090426
42737CB00009B/878